*Gifts
and
Giving*

Gifts
and
Giving

Lucy Fuchs, Ph.D.

ALBA · HOUSE   NEW · YORK

SOCIETY OF ST. PAUL, 2187 VICTORY BLVD., STATEN ISLAND, NEW YORK 10314

Quotations are from *Webster's New World Dictionary of
Quotable Definitions* by Eugene E. Brussell, © 1988, 1970 and
reprinted by permission of the publisher, Prentice Hall Business &
Professional Division / A division of Simon & Schuster,
Englewood Cliffs, New Jersey 07632.

Library of Congress Cataloging-in-Publication Data

Fuchs, Lucy.
    Gifts and giving / Lucy Fuchs.
        p.   cm.
    Includes bibliographical references.
    ISBN 0-8189-0601-4
    1. Christian giving.   2. Gifts.   I. Title.
    BV772.F83   1991
    248'.6 — dc20   91-11261
                                           CIP

Designed, printed and bound in the United States of
America by the Fathers and Brothers of the
Society of St. Paul, 2187 Victory Boulevard,
Staten Island, New York 10314, as part of their
communications apostolate.

Printing Information:

Current Printing - first digit 1 2 3 4 5 6 7 8 9 10 11 12

Year of Current Printing - first year shown
1991   1992   1993   1994   1995   1996   1997   1998

This is dedicated to Frank's family —
his mother and father, Frank and Frances
his brother and his family,
Joe, Lynne, Teresa, Leslie, and Joey
and his sisters, Mary Elizabeth and Rose Ann,
in gratitude for the gift they gave me,
Frank, my husband.

Table of Contents

Introduction

"It is in giving that we receive" (Prayer of St. Francis).
"It is more blessed to give than to receive" (Ac 20:35).

We have all heard statements such as these many times,
but many people don't really believe them. The newspaper
headlines daily seem to tell us that greed is growing in the
world. Again and again we hear stories of people grasping
what they can, no matter what the cost to others, society as a
whole, or the environment. In fact, in the past decade the
gap between the rich and the poor has grown, not only in
third world countries, but also in our own United States.

This is disturbing, but it is not surprising. The message
of giving cannot be learned by being told. It is something we
have to experience ourselves. People who have learned to
give freely find that it truly is more blessed to give than to
receive. It is not only blessed, but giving is wise. Giving is
truly the only way to receive and to have. Strange as it may
seem, the more one gives the more one has. Again this can
only be learned by experience.

When giving is spoken of, many people think that the
reference is only to the giving of money especially to
"charities," those organizations that always seem to be asking us for donations. Or people think of giving Christmas
gifts or other gifts to sometimes unappreciative relatives.
But giving is so much more than those two examples. Giving

of money is only one, and not necessarily the most important, part of giving. The giving of time may be more meaningful and much harder. Or the gift of work or energy, the doing of something for others. Or we may speak of the gift of helping another, or its opposite, and often equally treasured, gift of not helping. Or we may speak of the giving of compliments, which often people find hard to do, or even of constructive criticism, a most difficult gift to handle well. Or we may speak of the gift of listening or the gift of words or the gift of silence. Or we may speak of the gift of self, the highest gift of all.

All of these are aspects of giving. All of these are the ways in which our life is truly enriched.

Here, as in all important aspects of human life, our inspiration, our model, and our support for giving comes through God, especially as He reveals Himself to us in the Scriptures. He Who was perfectly happy alone and in Himself chose to give life to us, chose to share His life with us, and even chose to give His own Son. God Himself is the perfect Gift.

We will first learn to understand giving when we learn about the gifts given to us by God.

Gifts
and
Giving

Giving In The Scriptures

THE OLD TESTAMENT

The Gift of Creation

All of the Old Testament is, in a sense, a gift, since it shows the way the loving God interacts with His people, constantly giving to them and forgiving them, and building and rebuilding their lives. The first book starts appropriately with the first gift: the creation of the world, a pure love gift on the part of God. As the story goes, after He had created the world and all its contents, He created man in His own image, male and female He created them.

"God blessed them, saying to them, 'Be fruitful, multiply, fill the earth and conquer it. Be masters of the fish of the sea, the birds of heaven and all living animals on the earth.' God said, 'See, I give you all the seed-bearing plants that are upon the whole earth, and all the trees with seed-bearing fruit; this shall be your food. To all wild beasts, all birds of heaven and all living reptiles on the earth I give all the foliage of plants for food.' And so it was. God saw all he had made, and indeed it was very good" (Gn 1:28-31).

Thus from the very beginning it is made abundantly clear that God created all, all comes from Him, and all is good. God is the supreme gift-giver and any giving that we do must be modeled on Him. He gave good gifts to human beings and allowed them freedom to use them as they wished, even though, as He knew, they would often abuse them.

The Gift of the Covenant

Already with the Patriarchs, God gave His gift of a Covenant, an agreement with human beings. It is sobering to think of the great God Himself choosing to make an agreement with mortal beings. He told Abraham, "I will establish my Covenant between myself and you, and your descendants after you, generation after generation, a covenant in perpetuity, to be your God and the God of your descendants after you. I will give to you and to your descendants after you the land you are living in, the whole land of Canaan, to own in perpetuity, and I will be your God" (Gn 17:7-9).

Although God promised a mighty progeny to Abraham, his wife Sara was sterile and this was a source of great sorrow. God, though, gave Abraham and Sara a son, a true gift to them in their old age and the promise of a long line of descendants.

Children are most certainly a gift from God. They are the promise that we can be immortal; not that we ourselves will live forever on this earth but that our descendants will live on when we are gone. By giving Abraham and Sara a son only in their old age, God was demanding a great deal of faith from them. He was also making it clear that this child was set apart, a special child, a true gift and pledge of the Covenant.

Throughout the Old Testament we are confronted again and again with the way God keeps His side of the Covenant. He blesses His people, gives them children and

cattle, and victory in battle. Even when His people are unfaithful, as they often are, He is never unfaithful. This is the
giving God, whose gifts never depend upon our "deserving-
ness."

God's Gift of Selection

Throughout the Old Testament we meet the phenome-
non of God selecting certain people, again, not because they
deserve to be selected, but out of pure love and kindness and
freedom on His part. Jacob was such a person; so was
Joseph. Joseph's life was full of misadventure, but through it
all God was with him. In Egypt where he was sold as a slave,
he was falsely accused by his master's wife and thrown into a
prison. But, we are told:

"Yahweh was with Joseph. He was kind to him and
made him popular with the chief jailer. The chief jailer put
Joseph in charge of all the prisoners in the jail, making him
responsible for everything done there. The chief jailer did
not need to interfere with Joseph's administration, for
Yahweh was with him, and Yahweh made everything he
undertook successful" (Gn 39:21-23).

Joseph rose to the highest ranks in Egypt until the day
came when he could help his brothers and his father in their
time of famine.

Much later, when the Israelites were oppressed in
Egypt, God selected Moses to lead them back. Moses did
not want to be selected; he complained he could not speak
well; he worried that he would not be believed; he asked for
signs and miracles. God gave all that he asked and he was
able to lead the people out to the land that God had chosen
for them and given to them. What a gift was the gift of
land!

The Gift of Homeland

We in our industrial, non-agrarian society may not understand the powerful gift that a gift of land is. But we could ask the peasants of Latin American or those of Asia and Africa and they would tell us. Land is the most wonderful gift of all. Peasants yearn for land; they fight wars and revolutions to have their own small piece of land. When they have land, even a few small acres, they love to walk it, to feel the earth beneath their feet, to feel the soil and let it slide through their fingers. God's gift of land was a most precious gift to these people of Israel.

Although we may not be attuned to the love of the land, most of us are attuned to the love of a home. There is nothing more precious to us than our home, even for us Americans of whom 20% move every year. We long to come home to our own haven at the end of a long day at work. We feel comfortable in our homes. Our home is our castle; there's no place like home; home sweet home. We have mortgage-burning parties to celebrate that a home is truly ours. God gave the Israelites a home too, a precious place that was theirs. Never mind that it was small, rocky, and poorly endowed with mineral resources or water. It was to be their home; it was to be theirs.

The Gift of the Law

We find something in the Old Testament that we do not find in the New to any extent, and we may find it somewhat difficult to relate to. This is the concept that the Law given by God was a gift, a sign of His love. We today often see laws as interfering with our freedom, with restrictions put on us. Total freedom, we often think, would have been a greater gift. The ancient Israelites did not see it that way. They were aware of their personal freedom, also a gift from God, but the law was to them a precious sign of God's care for them. He interested Himself in their lives so much so that He revealed what would please Him and what would not. Some of the Psalms, in particular, Psalm 119, are hymns praising the wonder of God's gift of the Law.

We today may need to reexamine the concept of God's law as a gift. We have become aware of the problems of becoming too law-conscious, and Jesus himself warned us about putting the letter of the law ahead of the spirit. We also know that our relationship to God is supposed to be a love relationship, as one between friends, not a legal contract in the manner of which we relate to business associates. But even Jesus said that we are his friends if we do the things he commands us and his greatest law is the law of love.

The Gift of the Judges and the Prophets

Gideon was one of the early judges, selected for his position by God. Yahweh had told him, " 'Go in the strength now upholding you, and you will rescue Israel from the power of Midian. Do I not send you myself?' Gideon answered him, 'Forgive me, my lord, but how can I deliver Israel? My clan, you must know, is the weakest in Manasseh and I am the least important in my family.' Yahweh answered him, 'I will be with you and you shall crush Midian as though it were a single man.' "

But Gideon is still not convinced and so God gives him the signs he asks for.

Gideon was indeed weak among his people but that is often the sort of person whom God selects. And He does this totally gratuitously, the more to show His power. His selec-

tion of people is a true gift, and one that we would do well to
keep in mind. As we look around us and see the weak and
those whom we might call "losers," we may well find that
they are selected by God for some service for the rest of us.
What a beautiful gift of God, both for them and for us.

Samson was also selected by God to do His work. He
was strong physically, but he had other weaknesses. Yet the
fact that in spite of all his difficulties, he did God's work,
shows forth again, not the strength of Samson but of God.

Whenever the Israelites were in need of instruction,
prophets were sent to them. Some, like Isaiah, went en-
thusiastically to their call as a prophet; others like Jeremiah
held back. Some were brilliant and well-educated. Some
were poor farmers, like Amos. In each case they were sent by
the God of love who wanted to tell His people something.
Israel has been known for killing its prophets and stoning
those who warn them, but the message is always received by
some. The gift is given and there are at least some who see
the value of the gift.

Gifts to Women

In contrast to many stories of patriarchal societies, we
find stories in the Old Testament of God's gifts to women.
Ruth and her mother-in-law Naomi were so gifted, as were
Esther and Judith. All of these women in the Old Testament
were given special gifts for the good of their people. They
were instrumental in establishing the blood line or in saving
it. God is free to choose whomever He wishes, and He makes
no apologies when He chooses women. Very often, the gift
of the woman was her position as a mother. This was the case
of Hanna, the mother of the great judge Samuel. Hanna
prayed for a son and one was given to her. The prayer of a
mother for a son is often answered in the Bible; in many

cases the son born is beyond compare. Elizabeth, the mother of John the Baptist, closely resembles Hanna. These women asked with deep faith for a gift and they were richly rewarded.

The Gift of Kings

The Israelites wanted a king the way other nations had kings. God had always been their king, but they wanted one on earth. And so like the indulgent father He is, God gave them kings — first Saul, and then David and his sons. Saul, David, and Solomon each received special gifts from God. Saul was the great warrior and the first to be chosen. David was a great warrior also, as well as a poet and musician. Solomon was known far and wide for his wisdom.

Solomon, in return, chose to give a gift to God too. He was responsible for the building of the temple, the building that meant so much for the Jews. Their God was a mighty God, special among all the gods of the nations. He deserved the best of buildings, they thought. And they delighted in having a place, beyond the tents and the shelters, for the Ark of the Covenant.

There is, of course, much more to this story, but it was a loving gift of God to His people, and His people to their God, to have built such a wonderful temple. This temple of Solomon was later destroyed, but Herod the Great rebuilt it. It was Herod's temple that Jesus himself so admired and wept over. What a beautiful sight it must have been, and what it must have meant to the Jews.

The Gift of Poetry, Song, and Prayer

We have seen how the Jews loved the law, and saw it as a special gift of God. But all was not the law, and the law was not enough for all occasions. They were also gifted by God with the gift of poetry and song. David in his joy danced before the Ark of the Covenant. But many Jews sang and played the musical instruments of their day — flutes, string instruments, drums. They liked to sing of their joy in the Lord, of having been chosen by God as His own people, of having been given His law, of His mighty works in their lives and in their battles with other nations. But their songs were also expressions of their sorrows and their angers. God gave them the precious gift of using their emotional responses in their prayers to Him.

This is indeed a gift. Sometimes we almost wish we didn't have emotions; they often get us in trouble. And at times we meet people who live such orderly lives, with their emotions so well controlled or suppressed, that it is almost as if they were emotionless. But persons without emotions would not be true human beings. We are emotional creatures, made that way by God, and our emotions are what add zest and joy to life.

The Gift of Wisdom

The entire Old Testament is a book full of the wisdom that the human race has acquired through the centuries. Wisdom is so much more than knowledge or learning. It includes the ability to see beyond the superficial, to make right judgments, to follow the soundest course of action. To read the Scriptures is to learn wisdom. Sometimes the wisdom is portrayed in story form. At other times, in the rightly-called Books of Wisdom, advice is given in a straightforward manner. As we read such books, we are impressed with, first how true they are, and secondly how very simple. Yet, there is something in human nature which makes us often choose courses of action that are devious and not in our own best interest. We need to be able to put our wisdom into practice for the good of our neighbors. Sirach perhaps says it all:

"Many and wonderful are the gifts we have been granted by means of the Law and the Prophets and the others that followed them, an education in wisdom on which Israel is indeed to be complimented. But it is not enough merely for those who read the Scriptures to be learned in them; students should also be able to be of use to people outside by what they say and write" (Foreword).

And perhaps by what they do as well.

He goes on to say:

"Do not refrain from speech at an opportune time,
and do not hide your wisdom;
for wisdom shall be recognized in speech,
and instruction by what the tongue utters."

(Si 4:23-24)

and again:

"Do not be bold of tongue,
Yet idle and slack in deed." (4:29)

or again:

"Do not let your hands be outstretched to receive,
yet closed when the time comes to give back." (4:31)

The book goes on with sage advice, as do other parts of the Scriptures. These words of wisdom are too often forgotten and we must return again and again to the Scriptures to relearn them.

The Old Testament as a Whole

The Old Testament, as we have seen, is not only the story of the great gifts that God has given His people down through the ages and including us, but it itself, as the Sacred Scriptures, is a gift. We do not make the mistake some have perhaps made of using the Scriptures to replace the living presence of God, but we do see its tremendous value in our lives, as a source of great inspiration and life-giving power to those who read it. What a gift we have been given in this book itself. What a loving God we have who not only told us what He wants us to know but wrote it down for us, through His inspired writers, so that it would always be available for us.

THE NEW TESTAMENT

A Gift for a King

In Matthew 2 we read about the wise men who traveled afar to find Jesus. Verses 7-12 tell us: "Then Herod summoned the wise men to see him privately. He asked them the exact date on which the star had appeared, and sent them on to Bethlehem. 'Go and find out all about the child,' he said, 'and when you have found him, let me know, so that I too may go and do him homage.' Having listened to what the king had to say, they set out. And there in front of them was the star they had seen rising; it went forward and halted over the place where the child was. The sight of the star filled them with delight, and going into the house they saw the child with his mother Mary, and falling to their knees they did him homage. Then, opening their treasures, they offered him gifts of gold and frankincense and myrrh. But they were warned in a dream not to go back to Herod, and returned to their own country by a different way."

There are several interesting elements in this story. The wise men offered gifts to Jesus, and mysterious gifts they were. Herod also expressed his desire to go and offer homage, which he wanted the wise men to think would include gifts also.

Why does anyone offer a king a gift? Surely, of all people, a king does not need gifts. Poor people are needy but rarely do strangers come from afar and offer them gifts. But if those poor people should someday find themselves at a palace gate, they would want to have something to offer as a gift.

A gift for a king is never a gift given because the king is needy, although in Jesus' cause it was true. But a gift offered in homage is a token of the gift of oneself. To give a gift to a king is to say that one offers himself, his service, his life. In our democratic society we may have a difficult time grasping how the peoples of the past who lived in monarchies saw their kings. In many countries people believed that their king took the place of God on earth with the supreme power of life and death over his subjects. To offer him a gift in homage was to acknowledge that power. This may strike us as distasteful today, but it existed for many thousands of years in many countries.

Yet even today gifts are given to rulers, including our own President, who certainly does not have such supreme power. In this case we are accepting him as our ruler and showing our appreciation.

Herod, of course, had no intention of acknowledging any ruler other than himself. He wanted to find the child to destroy him. And when he was thwarted in his attempts, he reached further and destroyed as many boy children as he could.

Herod stands in sharp relief to the wise men. They came to give freely and lovingly to the child. Their gifts are listed as gold, frankincense, and myrrh, the three gifts often interpreted symbolically to mean an acknowledgment of

Jesus as a king, as God, and as man. But that is a later interpretation and perhaps unnecessary. Those gifts were simply costly gifts, of the type that one would offer a king. When we give gifts, our gift should suit the person to whom we give. When giving a gift to God or to a king in homage, our gift should be the best we have, poor though that may actually be. And this is true above all in giving our gifts to God.

Our Gift at the Altar

Much later, when Jesus was grown up, he preached his famous sermon on the mount. There he spoke of offering a gift to God at the altar. Matthew 5:23-24: ". . . if you are bringing your offering to the altar and there remember that your brother has something against you, leave your offering there before the altar, go and be reconciled with your brother first, and then come back and present your offering."

What a thought-provoking concept this is. Jesus wants us to realize that our gift at the altar really must represent ourselves. And our gift to God will not be acceptable if we are withholding our self from our brother. We cannot separate the two great commandments; they are part of the same. Love God with all your heart and your neighbor as yourself.

Generous Giving

Jesus went even further. Matthew 5:39-42: "On the contrary, if anyone hits you on the right cheek, offer him the other as well; if a man takes you to law and would have your tunic, let him have your cloak as well. And if anyone orders you to go one mile, go two miles with him. Give to anyone who asks, and if anyone wants to borrow, do not turn away."

Jesus wants us to be generous, to give without counting the cost. We are not only to give, but to give in, something far more costly. It is exactly what he himself does.

Jesus goes on to tell us how to give. Matthew 6:1-4: "Be careful not to parade your good deeds before men to attract their notice; by doing this you will lose all reward from your Father in heaven. So when you give alms, do not have it trumpeted before you; this is what the hypocrites do in the synagogues and in the streets to win men's admiration. I tell you solemnly, they have had their reward. But when you give alms, your left hand must not know what your right hand is doing; your almsgiving must be secret, and your Father who sees all that is done in secret will reward you."

We must give, but we must not give just so others will notice. We must give so that only our Father in heaven sees us for it is for Him that we are giving our alms. Our gift should be so secret that we barely know it ourselves. Jesus makes it very clear; if we do things publicly in order to be seen, we shall be seen, and that is the only reward we will receive.

This particular section is sobering to think about when we consider how difficult and perhaps how rare it truly is to give anything and be unnoticed. Lists of names and contributions are kept at our churches and at the offices of various charities. Plaques are put up to honor donors. For very large donors there are often other forms of public recognition, such as rooms, buildings, or even whole establishments named after them. Are these recognitions perhaps the sole reward for the contributions?

Jesus also made it clear that it was not the amount of money or goods that counted with his heavenly Father, but the intention and the sacrifice entailed in the offering. He explained as he watched people giving alms one day:

"As he looked up he saw rich people putting their offerings into the treasury; then he happened to notice a poverty-stricken widow putting in two small coins, and he said, 'I tell you truly, this poor widow has put in more than any of them; for these have all contributed money they had over, but she from the little she had has put in all she had to live on' " (Lk 21:1-4).

The Gift of Curing

Jesus himself gave the example of giving, but it was not money that he gave. Rather he gave according to the needs of the people.

Matthew 8:1-4 gives an excellent example. "After he had come down from the mountain large crowds followed him. A leper now came up and bowed low in front of him. 'Sir,' he said, 'if you want to, you can cure me.' Jesus stretched out his hand, touched him and said, 'Of course I want to! Be cured!' And his leprosy was cured at once. Then Jesus said to him, 'Mind you do not tell anyone, but go and show yourself to the priest and make the offering prescribed by Moses, as evidence for them.' "

What a touching story this is! The leper did not really ask to be cured; he simply stated his faith in the power of Jesus. And Jesus responded with his warm, "Of course I want to!" and he touched the man. That simple act of touching speaks volumes, for lepers were the untouchables. In fact they were supposed to warn everyone away wherever they went because to touch them, even accidentally, made whoever touched them legally unclean. But Jesus brushed all that aside and touched the man and with that touch cleansed him.

But he also, in accord with his own teaching, told the man not to tell anyone. It was a gift given in secret.

However, such a gift could not remain secret. It was not Jesus who told of it, but the recipient of the gift. As the leper found his health restored, he must have shouted out his praise of God and this God-filled man Jesus.

Jesus cured many people and all cures were personal and responsive. A cure was a marvelous gift to give and it was never given indiscriminately. Again and again we see Jesus responding in different ways to different people. Jesus "marveled" over the faith of the centurian, he cured Peter's mother-in-law with a touch, from others he drove evil spirits away with a word. The woman who had been hemorrhaging for years, a condition which rendered her unclean, thought she might just touch Jesus' cloak and she would be healed. She was indeed healed, but Jesus spoke to her with his comforting words, "Courage, my daughter, your faith has restored your health" (Mt 9:22).

The Gift of God's Call

As wonderful as his cures were, Jesus gave even greater gifts. To a select few he gave the priceless gift of a calling to be one of his close disciples. Matthew was called with the simple words, "Come follow me." Others were called more dramatically. To these disciples, Jesus gave his own gifts, "the authority over unclean spirits with power to cast them out and to cure all kinds of diseases and sickness" (Mt 10:1).

Gifts Given in His Name

With these gifts came also an invitation to follow the kind of life Jesus himself lived, one that would lead inevitably to the cross.

If we follow Jesus we find that he shares with us whatever is his, including the cross. But, on his side, he identifies with his followers. He says in Matthew 10:40-42:

"Anyone who welcomes you welcomes me; and those who welcome me welcome the one who sent me.

"Anyone who welcomes a prophet because he is a prophet will have a prophet's reward; and anyone who welcomes a holy man because he is a holy man will have a holy man's reward.

"If anyone gives so much as a cup of cold water to one of these little ones because he is a disciple, then I tell you solemnly, he will most certainly not lose his reward."

Jesus makes it very clear to us that whatever is given to another is given to him and he accepts it that way, even though it may be something as simple as a cup of cold water. Since the coming of Jesus, all giving has become sacred, if done in his name.

He also stressed the need and value of giving to the "little ones," "the least. He makes this abundantly clear in Matthew 11:25-27:

"At that time Jesus exclaimed, 'I bless you, Father, Lord of heaven and earth, for hiding these things from the learned and the clever and revealing them to mere children. Yes, Father, for that is what it pleased you to do. Everything has been entrusted to me by my Father; and no one knows the Son except the Father, just as no one knows the Father except the Son and those to whom the Son chooses to reveal him.' "

Jesus chooses the weak and the lowly to reveal his truths to. He is completely free in the giving of his gifts and he often gives to those whom the world would pass by.

Openness to Gifts

As Jesus gives the gift of his word, we find in a parable an important lesson. He is very liberal with his gifts, but some people neither recognize nor accept them because of their hardness of heart or their own dissipation with the things of the world. This is the image in the story of the sower and the seed (Mt 13). Jesus the sower throws out his seed rather randomly. Everywhere the seed lands, there is the possibility of growth, but only in the rich soil does the seed take root and grow strong. We need to prepare ourselves for the gifts of God and take them in.

We find that many people of Nazareth did not open their hearts to Jesus — he was the hometown boy whose family everybody knew, so how could he be a prophet — and so they were passed by in the giving of his gifts.

Wrongful Gifts

But there were others who did far worse. Herod was a man who had not completely closed his mind or his heart; he had a fear and respect of John the Baptist and perhaps a secret desire to live a life different from the one he had. But he was weak and engulfed in bad habits. In front of a large group of people he swore to give the daughter of Herodias whatever she would ask for. She asked for the head of John the Baptist and Herod gave it to her.

How strange to see that Herod made honoring his oath more important than the life of a human being. How sad to see that principles and life itself had to give way to Herod's standing among his friends. This kind of giving is poor giving because Herod rejected the real giving which would

have meant life — for himself and for John the Baptist.
Instead he chose to give death. Thus we see that giving, even
promised giving, must yield to a higher calling (Mt 14:1-12).
When Jesus heard of the death of John the Baptist he
seems to have been distressed. He wanted to get away and
spend some time alone, perhaps to mourn. But the people
would not let him. They followed him, hoping for cures.
And Jesus gave up his time, his privacy, and even perhaps
his grief, in order to minister to the people (Mt 14:13-14).
Then follows that most beautiful story of giving (Mt 14:15-
21).

The Gift of Bread

"When evening came, the disciples went to him and
said, 'This is a lonely place, and the time has slipped by; so
send the people away, and they can go to the villages to buy
themselves some food.' Jesus replied, 'There is no need for
them to go: give them something to eat yourselves.' But they
answered, 'All we have with us is five loaves and two fish.'
'Bring them to me,' he said. He gave orders that the people
were to sit down on the grass; then he took the five loaves
and the two fish, raised his eyes to heaven and said the
blessing. And breaking the loaves he handed them to his
disciples who gave them to the crowds. They all ate as much
as they wanted, and they collected the scraps remaining,
twelve baskets full. Those who ate numbered about five
thousand men, to say nothing of women and children."
What a beautiful story this is: Jesus' compassion, his
concern for the crowd, his desire to give food to the people,
his miracle which happened so quietly that the people
hardly realized that it was going on. His gift here was a gift of
food. Later he would tell his people to look for the higher
gifts, far beyond simple food. But Jesus knew well the im-

portance of giving people what they needed at the time. When people are hungry, they need food. And it was so much warmer on his part to give food than simply to allow them to go into the village to buy it.

The Gift to Outsiders

Another revealing story is the one in which Jesus was accosted by the Canaanite woman. She shouted at him, "Sir, son of David, take pity on me. My daughter is tormented by a devil." But Jesus would not even notice her. His apostles finally said, "Give her what she wants for she is shouting after us." In other words, give her what she wants just to get rid of her!

But Jesus still gave the appearance that he would not help her; it was not what he was called to do.

The woman would not give up.

Jesus said, "It is not fair to take the children's food and throw it to the house dogs." She retorted, "Ah, yes, sir; but even house dogs can eat the scraps that fall from their master's table." Then Jesus answered her, "Woman, you have great faith. Let your wish be granted" (Mt 15:22-28).

Here it seems that Jesus fully intended to give to her, but he wanted her to plead. And later in one of his parables, the story of the woman and the unjust judge, he told us precisely that. Ask, keep asking, and God will give. God wants to give to us, giving is His pleasure, but He does want us to ask.

Jesus' Gift of Himself

Again and again in the Scriptures we are confronted with giving. Jesus said to give and then give more. He himself gave examples of generous giving.

Eventually he gave the greatest gift of all — first his own body and blood, and then his life itself.

On the last night of his human life, Jesus gathered with his disciples for the supper feast of the Passover. Matthew tells us in stark simplicity:

"Now as they were eating, Jesus took some bread, and when he had said the blessing he broke it and gave it to his disciples. 'Take and eat,' he said, 'this is my body.' Then he took a cup, and when he had returned thanks he gave it to them. 'Drink all of you from this,' he said, 'for this is my blood, the blood of the covenant, which is to be poured out for many for the forgiveness of sins. From now on, I shall not drink wine until the day I drink the new wine with you in the kingdom of my Father' " (Mt 26:26-29).

Here is my body, he said, take it and eat it. Here is my blood, drink it. What more could he give? What more indeed.

But, as we see, on the next day he did give more, his actual life, in a cruel and painful death.

He had told his disciples, "A man can have no greater love than to lay down his life for his friends" (Jn 15:13). And that is what he chose to do, to give completely of himself.

There is no doubt that giving, in every sense of the word, is of the very essence of the Christian message. It was one of the things Jesus gave us the strongest examples of. And surely it is the one we must most strive to imitate if we want to be known as his followers.

Why We Should Give

Gifts for Many Reasons

We give gifts and time and services to others for many reasons. Sometimes we give out of necessity simply because we cannot choose not to give. This may happen at our work. What we give is called a gift, but truly it is not. At other times it is a matter of custom: a gift is expected at a wedding or graduation, for example, and we give to the honoree whom we barely know. Or we may give to get something in return. The salesperson who entertains a client and gives him gifts is looking to receive a large order and a large commission. Or we may give because we like to give. When we give, we feel good about ourselves. We are the generous Sir or Lady Bountiful. We have become philanthropists.

We may give money to charity to avoid paying income tax. We may give money to the church in order to be listed on the roll of donors. We may give to the poor person at our door simply to get rid of him. We may also give to him because we feel guilty if we don't.

Thus our giving has many reasons: necessity, custom, guilt, or the desire to acquire some reward or honor or business. We may even give so that we may be left alone.

Best Reason for Giving

The best reason and truly the only worthy reason for giving is out of love. We give to the poor, not because they annoy us with their presence but because they are our brothers and sisters in Christ and we love them. Any gift given for any other reason is not truly a gift. For a gift to be truly a gift, it must be freely given.

Perhaps much of our gift-giving comes with very mixed emotions, and often we are not fully aware ourselves of our reasons. But we do need to examine those reasons. We will find that a gift given so that we feel good is not good enough. There is certainly a good feeling that comes with giving to others, but we cannot give just for that reason. Then our giving is giving to ourselves more than to others. We can determine our motives along this line if we ask ourselves how we feel when no one even notices the giving that we have done, and no one says thank you. We can also ask ourselves whether, once we have given something, especially if it is over and above what we need (excess baggage, so to speak), we feel that we have accomplished all that we need to do. It is perhaps too easy to deceive ourselves: we have given to the poor, so we are good people. But have we really given of ourselves?

Guilty Giving

Guilt too is an unworthy motive for giving. This guilt comes from the fact that we have so much and others have so little. Just having so much makes us feel guilty. If we have been responsible for the poverty of others or if we have exploited them, we do need to feel guilty. But giving them a handout will not solve the problem. We need to face our guilt, ask forgiveness, and then try to right the situation. In such cases what is given to the poor is not a gift; it is a matter of justice.

Sometimes we feel guilty when we see the poor, not because we have exploited them or caused their poverty (for we never consciously have done so), but simply because their poverty disturbs us. We feel guilty having what they don't have.

There is a way in which such guilt is not misplaced. Although we personally may not have been responsible for exploiting the poor, our country or our class or our lifestyle may have something to do with the poverty of others. In such cases, it is much more difficult to right the situation. But awareness is the first step and this requires much more than guilt. What is required is an attempt to change things. We may need to alter our lifestyle. We may need to campaign for changes in our social system. In the meantime, we may help the poor, but this will not be a matter of guilt inducing us to give handouts. Again it will be an acknowledgment of the common brotherhood we share with the poor.

Required Giving

It is unfortunate that so often gifts are required, even demanded. These are not really gifts, of course, although they may come under that name. The word gift, as so many other words, has been cheapened through the use of commercials. Advertisers speak of giving people a free gift, "just for looking at their product." It is definitely not a gift. It is given only when the prospective buyer has paid for it with his time or attention or interest.

Natural Giving

The best gifts are those that arise naturally. It seems the normal and also most beautiful thing on earth that when one loves another person, he or she wants to give them a gift. We want to please that other person by offering them something. We put ourselves at his or her service in one way or another and our gift symbolizes that. Every time we use gift-giving to get something, we have cheapened the meaning of the word gift, and this includes such getting as relieving guilt, feeling good, or simply fulfilling obligations.

Only one reason is worthy of a gift and that is love.

To Whom We Should Give

We need to give to everyone. But this is a most thorny situation. Some people need things; others do not. Some, we think, deserve to be given to; others do not.

Giving to Family Members

To whom then should we give? First, we need to give to those who are closest to us, our families.

Husbands and wives need to give to each other constantly. They need to give love, concern, kindness, day in and day out. They need to think constantly of each other and constantly give.

Families are accustomed to giving to each other on special occasions. Christmas comes to mind immediately, as do birthdays, graduations, and weddings. But families have a way of being very ungiving sometimes of other things.

It is not unusual to find families in which the mother or father or children are very generous and giving to outsiders in terms of time, service, or care, and quite neglectful at home. Sometimes it is the father. He may be a counselor of some type or a coach or a boss. Those who work with him sing his praises as such a loving, caring, giving person. But he may not be like that with his own family. He simply does not have time or give time to them. It is as if he is off work at home and doesn't want to be bothered.

Or the mother may be the one who is involved in every social program in town. She is known far and wide for her projects and no doubt justly praised for them. But at home she is tired and irritable with her family, or her outside work takes her away from them just a little too often.

Or it may be teenage sons and daughters who get involved in social justice issues. They do not believe in the materialistic world that they accuse their parents of. They are idealistic, it is said of them. They want only the higher values. But that idealism does not extend to their own families. They have great concern for the poor and oppressed in El Salvador, Ethiopia, and China. They cannot be bothered by their father or mother or even bothersome younger brothers or sisters.

We cannot neglect our own families to give our time and talent to others. Our families need us, indeed, deserve what we can give them. Fortunately, only a few parents neglect their very young children, but it is not uncommon for families to neglect older children or spouses. They may be provided for physically, but many times family members are dying inside to be noticed and cared about and listened to. In some families, there is little or no conversation. Even meals are eaten to the tune of the evening news. Afterwards each person goes his or her own way.

Some parents will object that they would love to spend more time with their teenage children, but it is the children who are pulling away. This may well be true; teenagers experience a need to establish themselves as persons in their own right, and for that reason cannot allow themselves to be dependent on their parents.

And yet how badly they need their parents. The problem, contrary to what some parents think, does not start in the teenage years. If you do not talk with your eight-year-old, you will not be able to talk with your twelve-year-old, and you will not be able to talk to your sixteen-year-old. And teenagers have long since learned what kinds of things parents are not willing to discuss. They know when parents will become angry or rejecting and they will simply pull away from such confrontations. Or they will deliberately make such confrontations in order to show their parents that they are independent of them. What is happening is that children are growing up while parents are busy doing other things.

Or it may happen that married partners are pulling apart from each other as they each get engrossed in lives of their own. And this may especially be true of ambitious, career-oriented husbands and wives.

But giving time to each other, spending time together, talking, sharing, speaking even about the difficult-to-speak-of subjects, will help hold the family together. No one deserves or needs this kind of giving more than family members do.

Reaching Out Beyond the Family

It has often been said that charity begins at home and this adage must hold true under these circumstances. The second half of the adage is also true; charity begins at home, but must not stay there.

Besides giving to our families at home, we need to reach out to others. Just as a family in which the members have little sharing at home, but much outside the home is incomplete, so too its opposite, the family which is totally closed in upon itself. Members of a family must care about others. They must notice the needs of others around them.

It is an interesting and sad comment that many Americans do not know even their next-door neighbors' names. A generation or two ago, in many small towns across the country, everyone knew everyone. People did not bother to lock their doors; they knew things were safe with the people in their town. But today even small towns are changing. People are becoming more and more mobile, new people are moving in, perhaps of another race or class. People are suspicious and mistrustful of the new.

The old small town had many advantages, but there were disadvantages too. Everyone knew everyone and could, at times, be very supportive. But at other times, there was so much gossip, so much interfering in other people's affairs, that many people felt stifled. They could not be the persons they wanted to be in a small town which established its own norms and standards. The persons who marched to the beat of a different drummer felt compelled to leave and lost the support they may have needed.

The new urban and suburban life allows one to march to the beat of any drummer. It may also be a very lonely life, a life in which no one cares about anyone else. There have been some highly publicized cases of persons pleading for help and many people hearing and ignoring the cries; they did not want to get involved.

Psychologists tell us that loneliness and alienation are common among modern Americans. People feel isolated and believe that no one cares. Add to that the fact that families are often no longer intact and even when they are, they may not be supportive, and the reasons for the loneliness are quite evident.

But it doesn't have to be that way. Even in our concern for safety, which is one of the reasons people don't want to know their neighbors, police tell us that getting to know the neighbors, making friends with them, is one of the most important and effective ways of safeguarding one's home. That is why many neighbors are starting Neighborhood Watch Programs, which prove quite effective.

But it's sad that the need for safety may be the only way in which neighbors meet each other. And it's interesting that when Jesus talked about helping others, he used the word neighbor, the word we use for the person who lives next door to us. The Jews of his time were not sure what he meant. "And who is my neighbor?" one asked him.

Jesus answered by telling the story of the Good Samaritan.

Whom are we to help, we ask. Everyone. Everyone, especially those who need us. And who does not need us at one time or another?

What We Should Give

MONEY

When we think of giving, the first thing we often think of is the giving of money. For some people, this is the easiest thing to give. For others, it is the hardest. For many people, it is problematic.

Value of Money

We have a strange relationship with money. Many people value it totally out of proportion to its worth. Certainly we all need money in order to live in the kind of world we have today. We cannot simply barter our work for our food or clothing. But money has acquired a status far removed from its use, which is nothing other than to make it an easy medium of exchange to be used instead of the objects. Money has gotten so far away from that concept that we rarely think of it in those terms. It becomes an almost sacred thing.

Truly some people worship it as if it were a god. Some people want it in order to spend it conspicuously. Just having it is not enough; one must make it clear to everyone else that one has money. Others choose not to spend it but to save it, to hoard against a time which never comes. For them the money is valued in itself, not in the conspicuous use one can make of it.

Both of these types of people find it very difficult to give money. They have invested too much of their self-concept into their money. Their very sense of worth depends on how much money they have. And, unfortunately, our society reinforces this notion. Witness how differently rich persons and poor persons are treated. For those who view money in this way, to give it is to give too much of themselves, an interesting concept worth pursuing.

Being Asked for Money

But there are other aspects of giving money which are bothersome. People don't like to be asked for money. One of the biggest complaints that people have about religious groups and various churches is that "they are always asking for money." That criticism may even be true in some cases. One need only watch some television preachers to see how much time is spent asking for money to keep the show on the air or to build a church or other establishment.

Even in some mainline churches asking for money has, at least in the past, been so common that people expect it. And because they are constantly nagged for money, as they see it, they become stingy givers, thus reinforcing the need of the minister to ask yet again for money.

Charities too are always asking for money. Many of these charities have acquired a bad name. Just how much of the money they collect actually gets to the needy, in whose name the money is being collected? In some cases, the only people who profit from the donations are those who do the soliciting or those in administrative positions. It may happen that less than half of the money given actually trickles down to the needy persons.

Direct Giving

There is one way people can be sure that the money they give to charity truly goes to the poor, and that is to give it directly. One can go to a needy family and hand them money; one can give handouts on the streets to persons who are begging. But is it really that simple? How do the recipients of a cash donation, the needy persons, feel about themselves after they have been given something? Some feel insulted, even though they know well they need the money. Their relationship to the giver becomes one of gratitude, but it is a required gratitude, one that often destroys any kind of spontaneous friendship between the two. The handout on the street has its own problems. How does one know just how that money is used? It may likely be used for drink or drugs. And in both cases, the giving of money makes people dependent upon us.

Creating Dependence

This lesson needs to be learned by individuals as well as by governments. The U.S. government has often given money to poor countries (although rarely without strings attached) and it has caused upheaval in the lives and the economies of nations. An example is when an earthquake occurs in a Third World city. The U.S. and other countries ship food and supplies to the city. But the country area was not hit by the earthquake and when the farmers bring their food in to sell to the people, they find no one needs it; they have free food. Thus, what was done with good intentions, was harmful to other segments of the society.

On a personal level, we too do not want to give to others in a way that would create dependency. Surely it is better for others to learn skills, acquire jobs, and earn their own money than to live on "charity" — that beautiful word which has acquired a degrading sound. And yet and yet.

Our Need to Give Money

We do need to give money. All the money we have is meant to be put to good use. In a sense we don't even have a right to money that is over and above our needs. There is yet more: the one person in the Scriptures who was praised for giving money was the widow with her two mites who put in more than the others, Jesus said, because the others gave of their abundance and she gave of her substance. Even among Christians it is rare to find one who gives to the point where it actually costs him something; where he must sacrifice something he himself wants.

God's Response

In a way, God does not allow this to happen. As churches have been telling us for years, and as can only be learned through experience, God never allows people to outgive Him. Persons who learn to give generously to the church and to other needy organizations find that they always have enough. Somehow, when they need money, it is there. God has a way of providing for those who trust in Him.

And trust is what it is all about. God told us over and over again not to put our trust in money or in treasures. They can be devalued, they can rust and be destroyed through the years. Thieves may steal what one has; a fire may destroy it all. Even when the thief is apprehended and sent to prison, one's money is often not returned. Fires in a short time can destroy all that one acquired in a lifetime. And there comes a time when all one's material possessions mean little. When one gets old and sick, all that one has cannot bring good health or youth. And when one dies — unfortunately — relatives may fight over the possessions, or sell them off or they are simply thrown away.

Coming to Terms with Money

All of us have to come to terms with money and what money can buy. It can never be the symbol of our self-worth, although the world may use that symbol. But the world is fickle, and the person it praises today will be condemned tomorrow. Although the wealthy person may be honored at a public ceremony one day, often enough he will soon be vilified and dishonored. Since he is so much in the public light, his slightest transgression will be magnified in the press. The reporters who accepted the rich man's invitations to dine at his house and who wrote glowingly of its elegance, will also be the first to write disparagingly of the flaws in his personality.

Second, we must determine to give money. We must carefully choose the charities to which we will give. This will require prayerful thought and study. As we have seen, some charities may be more useful for the good of others than other charities. And, of course, some attract us more because they are more in line with the way the Spirit leads us.

We do not give out of a sense of guilt for having money. There need be no guilt at all, as long as our money is honestly gained. But give we must. And if it should happen that we are mistaken in our charities, that the organization or the persons to whom we choose to give turn out to be undeserving or even dishonest with the funds, it was still better for us to give than not to give.

Amount to Give

How much should we give? Some churches stress tithing as Biblically commanded. But it doesn't seem that God is a mathematician. He wants us to give freely and generously, not because we, so to speak, owe Him a certain portion of our pay checks, the way we owe the I.R.S. (which, incidentally, demands much more than tithes). Rather He wants us to give because He has given to us, and because we know that whatever He has given us was meant to be shared. He wants us to give generously, not in a begrudging manner, but overflowingly. He wants us to give cheerfully. He wants us to give because we acknowledge Him and Him alone as our God, not a golden calf or any other object.

TIME

Our Timed Lives

We are a very time-conscious people. Although our churches rarely ring out the time for prayer as they used to, important buildings in our cities often have huge clocks where everyone can see what time it is. Most offices have clocks in conspicuous places. Millions of us wear wrist watches so we can always be sure what the exact time is. In fact, a point of advertising for watches is how accurate they are. Radios regularly give the time. Television shows are timed to the exact second. And, as if all that were not enough, most cities have a telephone number which one may call twenty-four hours a day to find out exactly what time it is.

It isn't out of idle curiosity that we always want to know the time. Our lives are run by the hour. We may use an alarm clock to get us up in the morning. The sunrise has nothing to do with our rising. We eat breakfast at a certain time; we are expected to be at work at a certain time. We meet people by the clock, we work by the clock, we eat by the clock, we sleep by the clock. It can be truly said that time and clocks run our lives.

But there is never enough time.

"I haven't time," someone says, "I'm too busy."

"I would love to stay and talk with you," another says, "but I have an appointment. Got to run."

And on and on.

We may spend our whole days trying to keep pace with the clocks that relentlessly run our lives.

Is it any wonder that time has become such a precious commodity that it is one that people find most difficult to give?

Yet people need time. Children, the persons in our society who are the least concerned about time (until, alas, we train them), need much time. The baby wants, indeed demands, that we spend time with him. The small child is overjoyed when we take time to play with her. Children spend time in a different way than we do. We tend to think that if we do not use our time "productively" it is wasted. For a child, simply enjoying living is what time should be used for. Playing all day or exploring the wonderful world is a good use of time, although to a child the expression "use of time" is not even thought of.

But we think of that. We see ourselves as busy people with our lives scheduled full of what we consider important activities. When we find ourselves in a situation where we cannot use our time as we wish, we are often frustrated. We have great plans. Then we are caught in traffic which holds us up for an hour or more. Some people find such an experience totally exasperating, not to speak of wasteful of time. It is enough to throw their whole day off.

Time. Time. Time. The minutes and seconds slip away quickly. Clocks and watches are real and concrete, yet time itself is an abstract concept. Not only is it abstract, but it is remarkably flexible, in contrast to the rigid ordering of the timepieces we use.

Using Time

Everyone has the same twenty-four hours in every day. No one can truly say, "You have more time than I do."

When we say such things, we mean *unscheduled* time. But often we ourselves are responsible for the rigid scheduling of our time.

We need to use our time wisely, but we must break loose of the tyranny of time. And we must be able to establish priorities so that we can give time to those who need it.

Others need time from us. They need time to talk, time to share, time to simply be. And people should not have to ask us to "pencil in" their names on our schedules in order for us to have time for them.

As we establish our priorities we may consider the following:

Do we give top priority of our time to God and His work, or does He get what is left over?

Do we allow unscheduled time for enjoyment of the beautiful world we have been given?

Are we willing to shift or move appointments in order to take care of the needy around us?

Suggestions for Breaking with the Tyranny of Time:

1. Remember there is *nothing* that really must be done at a certain time. If we think certain things must be done, we have accepted the tyranny of time. If we remember that if we are sick or if we die, things will go on without us, then we can remember that any urgency is only relative.
2. Human needs must come ahead of work or manufactured needs.
3. Time wasters may include the following: television, frivolous reading, gossiping.
4. Time is well spent if we use it for listening to others and sharing with them, doing things for others.
5. We need to take the time to pray every day or we will find that we are simply running in circles all day. Prayer will give the needed focus and purpose to our lives.
6. We need time for ourselves too. We cannot give what we do not have and if we never take the time to relax or enjoy, to read or to sleep, to have a little space for ourselves, we will soon find ourselves burnt out.
7. It is worthwhile sometimes to spend large amounts of time on things that at first glance seem ephemeral. An example is the amount of time many people spend preparing for the Christmas holidays. It takes many hours to put up the Christmas tree and other decorations. It takes hours to send Christmas cards and to buy and wrap gifts. But those are a good use of time. Year after year Christmas is a magic time, the only time for many people when they are willing to spend time for others.

Ultimately most of us need to be much more relaxed about time and spend it more freely for others. There is probably no more precious gift we can give them.

HELP

"Can you lend a hand?" "Will you drive me to the store?" "How about helping me clean this place up?" "Will you help me with this lesson?" "Can you fix my air-conditioning for me?"

How often these requests come our way. And how often they are not really welcome requests. If we have shown ourselves willing to help once, we will no doubt be asked again. People who would die rather than ask us for money will not hesitate to ask us for help. This is all the more true if we are relatives. We all know that we are not likely to say no to relatives, even when we don't really feel like helping them.

What does helping consist of? Whom should we help? And most importantly, when should we help and when should we not help?

We can begin by understanding that giving people help by lending a hand to their work or doing their work for them is truly a giving, a type of giving that may cost much more than money or any other material thing. As such it is a valuable gift, often an invaluable gift.

Family Help

It is the kind of gift that we often give to relatives, even without being asked. When parents, children, siblings or even cousins are in need, it is normal for us to help them.

They are, in a sense, part of us, and we are perhaps doing for ourselves as much as for them when we help them.

Surely we need to help them. It is unfortunate that in our modern American society we have lost sight of some of the strengths and the importance of a close-knit family in which each member cares for the others and all care for each.

We have developed in far too many cases such an independence of spirit that people neither give nor ask for help unless they absolutely need to. And then it may be grudgingly given.

However, the strength of families is their mutual care and if we are going to revitalize American families this is where we need to start.

Giving help is rarely a problem when children are very young. They are not able to do many things alone and their dependence brings out the best in their parents and older siblings. Most are willing to help the very young child. As children get older they want greater independence but they still need the help of their parents. Parents make a big mistake if they will not help their children when they need help. The mother or father who helps the child with his or her homework will not only reinforce the importance of schoolwork, but will also build the bonds of mutual concern. The father who helps his child build a bird house or the mother who helps her child develop computer skills is doing the kind of helping that can be expected in a family and that is nurturing. So are the opposite kinds of help when the child is expected to help around the house and yard and with other work.

Children need to learn that helping is part of what they can do to build up the family. Very young children want to help with everything, although they are not often able to do it well. An excellent example is the little boy or girl who wants to wash the dishes. The child has to stand on a chair to reach the sink and mother holds her breath that he or she won't break any dishes. But she need not worry. Not many dishes will get washed; the child is likely to get totally absorbed in the suds and forget the dishes until the water is quite cold. But the child should not be discouraged from wanting to help. He or she should start with a few simple things and move into those which are more complicated. Parents need to take the time to show the child how to do things and they need to have the patience to put up with slow work, poor consequences, and lack of thoroughness. In time things will get better. Parents should be careful not to make the mistake of saying, "Forget it! I'll do it myself!" when it becomes too exasperating to watch a child's work. Patience and time are the keys to success.

As children get older, they need less help in some ways from their parents, but in other ways they need more. The kind of help older children need is the help and support to live the kind of life they want to live and know they should live, but which may be at odds with that of their peers. Here the help of their parents is essential. It is also most important that the parent be there to help them when and if they have failed.

In some families it seems that parents help least when teenagers need them the most. Such a situation may be when the young person has made a decision that is contrary to what he or she has been taught in the family. An example would be the case of the daughter who is pregnant or the son who has made a girl pregnant, or the teenager who is arrested for shoplifting, drunk driving, or abuse of drugs. Teenagers at these times in their lives need their parents' help the most, but it must be a particular kind of help. It cannot be the kind of help that increases dependence on the parent nor the kind that is reinforced with endless reminders that make the young person feel quite worthless. It also cannot be the kind of help that makes the young person feel that whatever he does is OK. This requires a difficult balance.

The teenager needs to know that his parents do not condone his behavior but they still love him. Their help is there to help him improve his life, not make it worse. But they will also insist that he learn what is probably the most important lesson he can learn at this point in his life: that all actions carry with them consequences and one must accept responsibility for one's actions and learn to live with the consequences.

Teenage years are also the years when young people want to help the least at home. In fact, they would rather not be at home if there is any place more interesting to go to; it doesn't even have to be more interesting, just different. Part of this is, of course, necessary. Teenage rebellion is part of growing up, of establishing one's own identity apart from one's parents. Refusing to work at home becomes a matter of principle to these young people.

Yet it need not be so. If the lines of communication have been established, if the parents have instilled in their children the idea of a family, children are more willing to help. This is what we do in a family, they begin to understand. It is not dad or mom giving orders; the teenager is not working for his parents. He is working for himself, for his group. And a group is something he does understand.

Not Helping

Is there ever a time when family members should not help each other? What about taking one's child home again after his second divorce at the age of thirty-four? What about one's ne'er-do-well brother-in-law who just cannot seem to hold a job? What about those grown-up children who want to enjoy life but don't want to accept any of its responsibilities?

It seems that family members need to look at these situations very honestly. Is it really helping someone to foster their dependency? Is it really helping them and you to make yourself a doormat? Is it lacking in charity to refuse to help?

Each situation needs to be decided on its own merits, but no one needs to allow others to take advantage of him or her, to the detriment of both parties involved.

And yet families, in the end, should be the last ones who will turn one aside. There should at least be a modicum of support; one can still talk to them, or visit with them, or loan them some money occasionally (perhaps insisting that it be repaid). A person who is always on the receiving end of help needs to think about himself too. Has he chosen to be a dependent child all his life?

Beyond the Family

People also need to be concerned about the needs of others beyond their families. We cannot be turned in on ourselves, caring just about our own. The world is full of needy people. One need only look around a little to find them. Any church, parish, community center has lists of persons who need help. Anyone who wants to reach out to others can easily find people who are needy. On such lists are persons who are old or ill and cannot leave their homes or who cannot do the work around the house or yard. Others are children who need to be cared for or retarded or otherwise handicapped persons, or veterans or abused persons. Needy people fill our cities. As you find one, you will quickly find many more.

Problems of Helping

Many people make it a point to help a needy person in one way or another every week. However, as life goes on, many middle-aged parents find themselves in the giving mode, not from outsiders, but from within their own families. They have aged parents who have great, perhaps daily need of them. They have college-age or even older children who have chosen to remain at home for more years yet. They may also have demanding jobs and great commitments at work and socially. Suddenly every day becomes a daily burden as they are drawn in all directions.

These persons would like to be kind and helpful, but they find that they are so tired so much that they feel resentful of anyone asking of them. When will they have time for themselves or when will anyone care about their needs, they wonder.

Again, persons need to look honestly at their circumstances and make some decisions. Being tired and resentful takes the joy out of living. Being all things to all people is impossible. These adults may need to insist on a change of behavior on the part of their children. They may need to get outside help for their parents. They may need to make some changes in their work schedules or plans.

The clue is when helping becomes burdensome. Helping done properly, should be joyous, enthusiastic, and always willing. When it is done this way, it makes for growth on the part of both the giver and the recipient.

Many people have learned this through experience when working in church programs. Their church is having a carnival and workers are needed, or people are needed to help at the dance, or to pack food for the poor, or to paint the social hall. The volunteers who come to help will find that they put in a full day of work, often hard work. Yet they will derive much satisfaction in doing something well and freely, in working with other generous-minded persons, in being a part of something beyond themselves.

It is impossible, some have said, to ever give more than one has received under such circumstances. And as long as persons do not help in order to receive they will receive much. It is one of the paradoxes of human behavior that one must give in order to receive, but that one cannot give only in order to receive.

One who adds up every minute of time and help given will not receive. He will constantly be comparing the help he gives others with what they give him, and in those cases, he will always seem to come out short. Thus in some parishes one finds that although people have seemed to give generously of their time and effort at a project, later they are resentful that someone received more credit than they did for the work. Giving must be done freely and with love.

Jesus himself provides the example of giving without counting the cost. He cared about others' needs, both spiritual and physical. When the people were hungry, he chose to provide them with food. But there was little food available, only a few loaves of bread and some fish.

He multiplied the bread and fish and there was enough for everyone, even many baskets full left over. This is generous helping, giving more than was needed and not even asked.

It is also significant that Jesus fled from the people after that, lest they make him king. He did not want people to follow him for his gifts, but for himself. But he wanted to help people. He told his followers again and again to ask of him and he would help. He made promise upon promise to help. And he keeps his promises.

Helping others, therefore, in the myriad spiritual and physical ways that we are constantly being asked, brings us closer to that great helper.

WORDS

What are Words?

Words. What value are they? Is it true that talk is cheap? Talk without action some will say, profits nothing. Sticks and stones may break my bones, but names will never harm me.

How wrong these concepts are. Words are the most powerful things in the world.

In the beginning, we are told, was the Word. And the Word was with God and the Word was God. It was through the Word of God that all was made. Jesus Himself is called the Word of God.

What a precious gift God gave us in His Son, the Word. And also what a precious gift He gave us in His word in the Scriptures.

We also can give precious gifts when we give words.

It is difficult to overestimate the power of words. Armies move forward in deadly action, bombs destroy cities and towns, people harm each other in many ways, and all because of words. On the other hand, people reach out to each other, love each other, care for each other, also all because of words.

It has been often said that actions speak louder than words. That is true, yet the words are there first. The problem is not the words themselves. It is the actions that do not follow or follow falsely. Yet in the beginning is always the word.

Instinctively we know the power of words. As young babies, adults already talk to us in words, even though we cannot yet understand them. But we respond to those words; they are our communication. Words accompanying the gentle touching and caressing of our mothers reach us and mark us for life.

Shaping Our Lives Through Words

Linguists in their study of words have concluded that we even shape our thoughts through our words. Putting our ideas into words not only makes them clear for other people; it also makes them clear for us. This is so true that perhaps half of all the work done by psychologists and psychiatrists with troubled people consists simply in having the people verbalize their problems and feelings. Once they can do that, the problems become manageable.

When we go to medical doctors when we are ill, we begin to feel better as soon as the doctor has labeled our illness. Once it has a name, we know what it is, and we can learn how to cure or at least control it. If just naming an illness or verbalizing a problem can help in solving it, how much more can carefully selected words do in building relationships.

People who say such things as "Talk is cheap," mean, of course, that it is easy to talk but never do anything. But talk is not cheap. It takes a great deal of effort to say the right things. It takes training and practice and deep sensitivity to know the words that others need to hear.

Many people are hungry to hear a kind word. Many people are dying for someone to say, "I love you." "You are

OK." "I forgive you." "I miss you." "Thank you." "You are very special," and all the rest.

Family Words

Often enough it is one's own family who neglect to say these words. Family members often take each other for granted. Mother or father work hard all day for each other and for the family and no one says, "Thank you." They are only doing what is expected of them. Children, too, are often neglected. The mistakes they make will be quickly pointed out, but their good efforts will be overlooked or they may receive a half-hearted compliment: "Good school work, Jimmy; now if you could just remember to clean your room."

There is a tradition in our culture of the "strong silent man," the one who says little but performs mightily. This tradition needs to be looked at, if indeed it is not more myth than reality. Picture the silent cowboy who went to town to woo a young lady. It must have been a difficult courtship; he never knew what to say. And the marriage would have been difficult too, with the young woman pining for words of love and concern.

All women are perhaps romantic and they want to hear words of love. Men too want to hear such words. Yet many people are totally inept at such language; they may even have a disdain for it. And it is possible to use words that are cloying and annoying rather than expressing strong sentiment. Perhaps we need to practice how to say the right things.

It is interesting that many people say, "I love you," to small children, but not nearly so many say those three most important words to teenagers. What has happened? They are still the same people. Somewhere along the line the loving words have gotten lost in the shuffle of so many other concerns. It is easy to say, "I love you," to an innocent child who cannot be held responsible for his behavior. It is much more difficult when the teenager stays out too late, uses the car in a reckless manner, has a room that requires a permit from the Board of Health to enter, and who can never remember to help around the house. And yet the teenager needs the loving kind words as much as the child does. His way of asking for it is just so inept.

The teenager, in his desire for independence, often pushes away the persons whom he needs the most. And then he wonders why they neglect him. He will understand all this someday. In the meantime, parents need to be patient and not settle for only negative words.

Positive and Negative Words

Many people are far more negative in their words than they realize. Some don't even like it when others say such things as "Good morning," or, "Have a good day." They don't feel like a good morning and what right do you have to tell them to have a good day. Some say they don't like the relentlessly cheerful person. But isn't it amazing that sometimes we are more tolerant of the relentlessly grouchy person than we are of the positive sounding one? They are more realistic, we think. As if, if we truly were aware of the world, we would see only the bad.

The world is made up of both good and bad, happy and sad occasions, and we can choose which we will concentrate on. The idea that negativism is realism and positivism is fantasy is the thinking of a negative person. We choose to be happy or sad. Optimistic persons are not unaware of the dark side of human life; they simply choose not to dwell on it. They choose to look for the good. And those who look for the good will certainly find it.

Whether we choose to use positive words or negative words, our attitude is contagious. By both attitudes we influence those around us. Some people bring joy and happiness wherever they go. Others bring gloom. "I was feeling good today, until you started to talk." Or "I was feeling so blue, but now I feel much better. I am certainly glad I talked to you."

The latter is, of course, the attitude we want to give others. Our words may bring enlightenment, or joy, or an answer to a problem, or a moment of laughter, or encouragement, or hope, or maybe just an interesting interlude.

We can never do enough to develop our facility with words. We need to make our voices pleasant, the kind of voice people want to listen to. We need to use our skills to be able to tell an interesting story, one we know will interest others. It is not enough for someone just to say, "I was never good with words."

We can all be good with words. Indeed we must be. It is our major source of communication, of building relationships, and it, like all skills, comes with practice.

Magic Words

It is interesting that when stage magicians perform, they always have magic words that they say, the words that make something happen. Words are indeed magic. They have the three elements of magic: power, mystery, and just plain fun.

Words are so powerful, as we have seen, that they can totally change one's attitude, one's feelings about something, one's self. Words make things happen.

But words are mysterious too. They always mean more than they seem on the surface to mean. That is because words are invested with feelings, memories, and connotations, far beyond their dictionary definitions. Family words said to us by relatives bring back all the joys and securities of our childhood. Words spoken by loved ones delight us anew, just as words that were used in the past to frighten us may still do so.

And finally words are fun. We enjoy well-spoken words, jokes that are based on plays of words, clever comparisons, and rhymes and riddles. These, too, are a part of the gift of words, one of the most precious gifts we can ever give other persons.

The Gift of Self

We have all heard this expression, the giving of self, and we all know it is something to be striven for, something to be admired, something that a committed Christian ought to do. But what precisely does it mean? And, more important, how does one do it?

It is harder to define the giving of self than it is to see it in action. We know and have seen people give of themselves. Jesus, the great exemplar, completely gave of himself when he lived and when he died for us.

We can think of many examples of missionaries who gave their entire lives for people of another country, or people living today like Mother Teresa who has spent her life on the streets of India caring for the sick and dying. These people truly have made the gift of themselves. But what about some closer, more at-home persons?

We see them too. Have you ever seen a teacher who was totally dedicated? Who prepared each class well, who cared about each student, who truly poured out himself for the class. Just what he does may not be easy to catalog, but we know it when we see it.

The same is true of the man and woman who care for their family that way, who are totally dedicated to providing a good and happy life for each member. Or a person may give himself for his work; he may give himself to build up the company. We see this all around us.

Self-giving as Commitment

Yet it is quite possible to go through life and never give oneself to anybody or anything. It is quite possible to live totally for oneself, never to make a true commitment to another person, never to find anything in the world that one wants to be a full part of. But it is the saddest thing on earth when this happens, because we only become our full selves when we give ourselves totally to something beyond us.

"Unless a wheat grain falls on the ground and dies, it remains only a single grain; but if it dies, it yields a rich harvest" (Jn 12:24). The grain must die. One must give oneself. We all must die for others, if we want to live and grow.

What this means in actual practice is that we must find what we are called to do in life and give ourselves to it. We must make a commitment body and soul. That is the only way we will ever be full human beings.

Antoine de Saint-Exupery, the French author of such books as *The Little Prince* and *Wind, Sand, and Stars*, was the pilot of a small plane in the days when such flights were often dangerous. He was asked why he was willing to risk his life for something so unimportant as getting mail delivered on time.

It is not the mail that he was committed to, Saint-Exupery explained. It was his commitment to what was his responsibility. For it is accepting and carrying out responsibility, he said, that makes us truly human. And it is the only way we can ever reach maturity.

It is necessary to give ourselves, for this is truly what makes us ourselves. And it is the source of a great deal of happiness.

Human beings are constructed in such a way that they cannot live for themselves, even if they want to, even when they think that is what they are doing. Living for oneself ultimately means destroying oneself.

What keeps us from truly giving ourselves? Is it that we are afraid of being taken? Do we think that if we give totally of ourselves, we will have nothing left? Or we may find ourselves old someday, too old to try something new and find that what we chose as our commitment wasn't a good choice. That may indeed happen, but such a commitment is infinitely better than never having made any commitment. It is only in giving that we receive, only in giving totally of ourselves that we are ourselves. The person who is too afraid of being taken is the one who will never learn to give.

How to Give Oneself

The following are suggested as ways to give oneself:

1. Whatever you are engaged in, put yourself into it. Do it with competence and commitment. This is true whether one is arguing a case before the Supreme Court or babysitting some children. Doing things only halfway or not giving a task one's full attention ultimately means that one has concluded that the task is not worthy of one. If that is the case, what is worthy? Are we always waiting for the big important task that will fall to us one day and to which we will totally give ourselves? We may find that we will wait a long time or forever for such a task. Those big important tasks, like big important roles given to actors, are given to those who have performed well in lesser tasks.

2. Reconsider the concept of importance. What makes a task important? Most of us think in terms of ultimate results. A task is considered important if it has long-reaching effects. This is undoubtedly true. Surely, a surgeon knows

that his performance may mean life or death to his patient. Or a judge may make a decision in court which will determine the entire future of a criminal. But little tasks have important results too. One by one they establish the kind of persons we are.

3. Be present when you are present. It was said of Thomas Merton that when you were with him, he had the facility of treating you as if you were the most important person in the world, that there was no one he would rather spend some time with. What a marvelous ability this is. He was truly present to those who spoke with him. The gift of our presence is a true gift of self.

4. Finally give yourself, not with an intensity which disturbs others, but with calm and joy. We all like to be around people who are happy and content with themselves, who know who they are and where they are going. These persons give of themselves, but they also give strength and inspiration to others who have contact with them. They make others want to share their commitment. It is the unction of their joy that is attractive. A harsh, cold and driving ambition frightens us away. But that which is grasped with joy and enthusiasm inspires us.

Giving oneself is true and total giving. "Freely have you received; therefore, freely give" (Mt 10:8). Give until you think you have nothing left to give. And you will see you always have more. Your self becomes unending.

A final word must be said concerning the idea of burning out. Some will say that it is possible to give and give until there is nothing left to give, and that one must be revitalized before he has enough to give again. This will not happen if he gives appropriately, meaning that he not only loves his neighbor as he loves himself, but that he loves himself as he loves his neighbor. He will allow himself to rest, allow himself to enjoy some quiet time, some time apart. Otherwise, instead of giving cheerfully and lovingly, he will find himself resenting his giving because he is perhaps too tired, either physically or mentally.

Giving of oneself is meant to be a joyous giving, not a burdensome one.

Not Giving

"I never give Christmas gifts," the man said, "and I don't want anyone to give me any. I don't believe in presents."

And he didn't. When his friends were ill, he never sent flowers. When birthdays came, he never remembered. When Christmas came, he studiously avoided all Christmas shopping.

A few people still gave him gifts, but he never thanked them; he just let them know that he didn't believe in gifts. He considered himself self-sufficient. All that gift-giving was a waste of time and money, he thought.

And then he wondered why he was so lonely.

Interdependence

Not to give is to deny our interdependence on each other. Not to give is to want to break our bonds or to refuse to create bonds that hold us together and complete us.

There is no doubt that there are many problems with gift-giving, but the problems are in the misuse of giving rather than giving in itself. One may use gifts as bribes or as ways to force others to give gifts. There are also examples in history of gift-giving customs which actually forced others into penury. But giving is a powerful human instinct.

Learning to Give

It is most beautiful to see a child when he or she first gives a gift to a parent. Often it is something simple, like the child who has candy and wants to give part of it to an adult. It may even be a piece of candy which has been tasted and found to be worthy of the adult. Or it may be the picking of the top of Mother's flowers, the pride and joy of her garden. Psychologists tell us that when the child starts giving gifts, he is starting to mature. He is beginning to move out of the natural egotism that he is born with, in which he believes that the world revolves around his needs. By giving his first gift, he is reaching out of that and acknowledging the existence of other human beings who also have needs.

Through our childhood we are slowly being brought to understand that we are not alone in this world and that we all must work together to make our happiness. The well-brought-up child will slowly begin to take as much joy in another person's happiness and satisfaction as he does in his own. When we want to make others happy, we have reached a state of maturity.

It is this concern for the needs of other persons that creates those bonds we all need. "Bonds" is perhaps an unfortunate word, although it is difficult to find another appropriate one. The idea of bonds conveys to us the idea of something restricting or prohibiting behavior. But that is less than half of what bonding means. The deepest meaning of bonding is in its concept of being connected to others, having a support group, having persons in our lives who care what happens to us. No one, even so-called loners, can live happily without some bonds.

Babies naturally bond with their parents or other caretakers. They learn to want to please these people, they want these people to be happy to be with them and they delight in their presence. These are the first and perhaps the deepest bonds.

Bonds are created in the giving and receiving of gifts. But if it is not only more blessed to give than to receive, it is also often easier.

Some people do not want to give nor to receive because they do not want to be, as they say, "beholden" to others. In this case, being the recipient of a gift causes the problem. These people do not want to feel that they must do something for anyone else. This attitude often reflects something deep in Americans, the desire to be independent, to walk alone, to do our own thing. It is a human need to want to accomplish things on our own. But there is another complementary human need, that of belonging, of being aware of how much we need other people, how often we should be "beholden" to them.

Reciprocal Nature of Gifts

Not giving and not receiving removes the connectedness of our lives.

Obviously we are not talking here only of material gifts. There are other gifts — the telephone calls, the visits, the thoughtful compliments, the words of appreciation. Each of these gifts call out for a response in kind too.

The person who does not and will not give is the person who is lonely. He may be hurting from his loneliness, but he is afraid to reach out and take the chance of connecting with others.

He may have been hurt as a child. He may never have been given anything as a child. Or gifts had to be earned at great cost. Or they were always given grudgingly, and he was made to feel unworthy of them. With this kind of background, he will withdraw from an engagement which is so fraught with perils, as he sees it. Better to close off oneself, he thinks, than to suffer the pain of vulnerability again.

Others who do not give were not deprived as children. They simply never learned to be unselfish. Perhaps their parents catered to their every whim. This is so sad, because one of the most valuable lessons parents can teach their children is the joy of giving and sharing. Selfishness is the kind of behavior which is most deceptive. It makes one think that if he is selfish, he will have more. He will keep everything for himself and no one else can use it. But he will find that what is selfishly kept remains alone. Given away and used by others, it multiplies and grows and he has much more. The only way to understand this is to do it.

When St. Francis and his followers gave away whatever they had to the poor, they did not feel deprived. Instead they felt free and full of joy. They learned the valuable lesson that possessions themselves never bring happiness; only in their use, including giving them away, can happiness come.

Twelve Things To Give

1. *Give an ear.* Listen. Let the others tell you that old story one more time. Let them explain once more why they did what they did. Listen. Listen to what they are really saying underneath the words. Listen to the pain. Listen to the pride. Listen to the suffering. Listen to the happiness. Listen. Listen. Listen. Don't spend your listening time thinking what you will answer when they stop talking. Don't spend your listening time thinking about your plans for the rest of the day. Don't interrupt. Don't tell stories of your own. Ask questions, but ask only questions that relate to what they are talking about. Open your heart as well as your ears.

2. *Give trust.* This is a gift that may sometimes be the hardest gift of all to give. Parents know that they must take the chance that the trust they give their children may be betrayed. Yet they need to give their children trust or their children will never mature. Children also need to give trust to their parents, that the parents who sometimes forget or misunderstand things will not make major mistakes and will never forsake them. We need to give enough trust to our friends to tell them things about ourselves, and allow them to tell us things about themselves. We need to have enough trust in our spouses to entrust our happiness to them. We need to have enough trust in God to let Him take over our lives.

3. *Give material things.* Give gifts to people, valuable things, inexpensive things, any kind of thing. The issue here is not that other people need things so much as we have the need to give. There is nothing sadder than a person who tries to hold on to what he has so tightly that he crushes it. We cannot really keep anything. It is like holding water in our hands. Give anything and everything away. What we have is only lent to us for awhile. The day will come when it will all be taken from us. Even if it is pried from our cold dead hands, as they say. But it will be so pried. We cannot keep anything. No material thing lasts. We can only use it, put it aside, or give it away. And giving it away makes it doubly valuable.

4. *Give joy.* Some, they say, spread joy wherever they go. Others spread joy whenever they go. What makes the difference is in their attitude. The former enter a room, pleased to see the others who are there. He or she notices the others, compliments them on what they are pleased with, commiserates with what they are sad about, and talks about interesting, amusing, or perhaps profound ideas. These people are welcome at any party. Anyone would like to have them around. They smile and make others smile. They entertain but their entertainment is never vicious. It is the kind of entertainment that makes others feel good. These joyful persons bring out the good in others, mostly by simply recognizing that good. They look beneath the surface and see the good person waiting to come out. They entice him out, and the room erupts with joy.

5. *Give beauty.* Most of us will never be known as gifted artists or musicians, but we can all give beauty in one form or another. We can appreciate what is beautiful around us and share that with others. A husband left his wife a note which

she found when she came home late from work: "I heard a whippoorwill tonight at 7:10." Sharing that moment of beauty spoke deeply of his love for her.

6. *Give thanks.* Say "thank you" to everyone who does anything at all for you. Thank the waitress who brings you your food. Thank the trash collector who picks up the trash. Thank the person who asks about your health. Thank the secretary who takes messages for you, or types letters for you. Thank the mailman who brings welcome letters, as well as bills and junk mail, to you. Thank the child who picks a flower for you. Thank your parents for bringing you up. Thank your spouse for marrying you. Thank your children for being your children.

At a language school in Mexico, students are told that if they say *Gracias*, thank you, a hundred times a day, that will not be enough. Two hundred times a day would be a good start.

7. *Give compliments.* Some people never give compliments. Perhaps they were not brought up with compliments or perhaps they were told that most compliments are insincere and that people who give compliments always want something. It is true, of course, that compliments can be insincere, but there is no reason why they must be. Everyone needs and wants compliments, even those who deny they do. We need to compliment people on what they consider their best points, on what they want us to notice. But we also need to use compliments to point out to others some of the good qualities they possess that they may not be aware of.

The reverse of this is the need to accept compliments graciously. A simple "thank you" is best, but a word of appreciation is also appropriate. What we do not want to do is to deny the compliment, to pretend that we do not have the quality.

8. *Give advice.* There is an old adage that goes like this: Advice is seldom heeded. Those who want it don't need it. Those who need it don't want it. But there is a time and a place to give advice. Certainly we do not give advice when people do not want it. And even when they want it, it must be given appropriately. No one can make a decision for another person. Each person must live his or her own life. And yet sometimes a gentle word of advice is a true gift. We have gotten to be so independent that we forget that human beings are meant to learn from each other. We do not need to all make every mistake in order to learn from it. With a little help from those who have experienced what we have not, we can profit from advice. Advice, however, is like some spices. Use only very little.

9. *Give ideas.* We get a wonderful idea and perhaps we immediately want to patent it or get a copyright on it. Ideas, we think, are truly our own and we are distressed to think that someone else may use them. But ideas in themselves are rather easy to come by. It is how ideas are used that makes the difference. Again we need not be afraid to share ideas. If someone else can put them to better use than we can, so what?

10. *Give forgiveness.* Extend forgiveness to everyone for everything. Let go of all past hurts and offenses and sorrows and pains. Forgive and forget. Free yourself from everything. Let go completely. Take everyone back into your friendship no matter what happens.

11. *Give laughter.* What a precious gift is the gift of

laughter. How much happier schools would be, if children and teachers could laugh together. How much happier homes would be if people would develop their sense of humor and appreciate the incongruity of circumstances. How many problems could be solved if people could laugh and enjoy together.

A sense of humor, like all skills, can be developed. This gift, like the gift of forgiveness, requires one to let go of seriousness, letting go of all the harshness and sternness of life. If we all took ourselves less seriously, life could be so much better.

12. *Give a prayer.* No matter what else happens, we can always pray for others. Prayer is a best and final weapon. We can solve all the problems of the world with a prayer. With prayer we can reach out to everyone. This gift of prayer is the best gift we can give anyone and it is one that we always have available.

Ten Ways Always To Give

1. *Give generously, more than is asked.* Don't be afraid that you will be giving too much. It is, of course, possible to give too many material things to certain people, children, for example, or others whom one will make dependent. But giving itself should always be generous. Generosity is an attitude, a spirit, more than the amount given.

2. *Give cheerfully, making the other think that giving to him is your greatest pleasure.* Smile when you give, make light of any sacrifice it may have cost you. Joke with the person who is receiving the gift.

3. *Give thoughtfully, trying to give the other what the other really likes.* Such giving requires an attempt to get inside the other's way of thinking. But once we know other people, we know what they like. It is even possible to give them things that they will like, things they never would have thought of asking for. It is the way some parents have of awakening new interests in their children.

4. *Give in such a way that you downplay your part.* The purpose in giving is not to make others beholden to you. Nor is it to create dependence upon you. Unfortunately so much giving on a national or international level degrades

the recipient, makes him or her, or the whole country, dependent, and destroys their own initiative. Give in a way that builds up the other.

5. *Give anonymously if you can.* Your gift, given in secret, will be seen by God. Now obviously there are many times when anonymous giving is impossible, but there are many times when it is not. Such giving is part of the mystique of Santa Claus. He is a sort of mysterious figure who gives Christmas gifts. Parents, those most loving gift-givers, are thus anonymously giving.

6. *Give as to the Lord Jesus.* He told us himself that what is given to others, he accepts as given to him. He even said that he would accept even a cup of cold water, if given in his name. But looking at it from the other side, how would we give gifts to Jesus, if we had the opportunity to do so in person? We would give generously and lovingly, the best of whatever we had. And so it must be in whatever we give. Gifts given to others should not be things that we are trying to get rid of.

7. *Give frequently.* Be the kind of person who never fails to give to the other person. Gift-giving should not be limited to the special occasions like Christmas and birthdays when gifts are expected or required. Gifts should be given whenever the spirit so moves us.

8. *Give whether or not the other ever thanks you or responds in any way.* This is hard to do and many people decide after a while that they will no longer give to people who never write thank you notes. On the side of the recipient, not to write a thank you note is a serious breach of courtesy. But the giver may need to be a little more forgiving than that. It is all a

matter of why we give. When we give blankets to the poor and they do not thank us for them, what is the reason? Is it because they do not like or want the blanket? Probably not. If they are cold, a blanket is most welcome. But perhaps they have never been taught to be grateful. Or perhaps they resent the fact that we, so much better off, can afford to give away a blanket; we have ten more at home unused. Or perhaps they hate the second class position they are placed in by being in need of a blanket.

When a niece or nephew or child does not say thank you, the situation is different. Chances are they have not been so taught. But there comes a time in everyone's life when they can no longer blame lack of training. They must learn to do it themselves. However, it seems that parents or others ought to ask the recipients if they had received the gift and express concern since they had not been heard from. They need to be shaken from their lack of gratitude.

9. *Give when gifts are expected, but give also when they are not.* Give when the person needs something. Give when he or she doesn't seem to need anything; especially, if they say they need nothing. What they may need then is not something material, but, as we have seen, non-material gifts are every bit as important, usually more so.

10. *Give with some style and class.* If you are giving gifts, wrap them well and make them beautiful. If you are giving a compliment, smile and use the most appropriate words. If you are thanking someone, another form of gift, do not just sign a thank you card; write your own well-chosen words. Let your giving style be as unique as you are.

Results of Giving

When we give we receive. When we give much, we receive much. Giving creates a kind of order in the universe, a balance, a reciprocal action. To give is to receive more than we can ever give. Giving means receiving; it also means both freeing and bonding us. It takes away from us and in return fills us with joy.

First Result: We receive

We receive when we give. People who give generously tell how they always receive more than they give. If one gives a few hours a week to a service project, he will feel that he has contributed some time and energy, and he will find himself repaid more than he gave by the new friends he has made, by what he has learned, by the knowledge he has that he has helped improve a bad situation.

People in business know that in order to make money they have to spend money. They have to advertise, they have to treat others, they have to give more than expected. Customers willingly return to stores where they are well-treated. Customers like the salesperson who is generous with his time and help, even if they don't buy from him at that time. Later they will.

Business people also know that they must be willing to give to community and charitable causes, not just to write it off on their income tax, but because they need to be a part of the community. They have much to gain by giving and they do gain.

We must give to receive spiritually too, but we don't give just to receive. Instead the receiving follows naturally and it is amazing how well rewarded we are for whatever we give. But for this to happen, the giving must be willing and generous. Giving grudgingly is not real giving.

Second Result: We become free

We free ourselves when we give. To give away items to others is to free ourselves from relying on any natural thing. All human things, all material things will pass away. Getting too involved in them, valuing them too highly, clutters up our lives, pulls us down. Without so much clutter we are free to be ourselves as we are, without objects interfering.

All material things require much care. If we own a house, it needs constant maintenance or it will soon be run-down. If we own a car, it cannot serve us if we do not care for it. If we own expensive jewelry, we must keep it under lock and key if we want it to be safe. Silver must be polished, money must be banked, and paperwork on accounts must be supervised. The care of our possessions can take all of our time so that we have little time left to contemplate nature and enjoy the simple things of life. Giving away items can free us from a very real slavery.

Third Result: We create bonds

We create bonds when we give. This may sound like a contradiction of what was just said, but giving both frees us and ties us. But these bonds are the kind of bonds we want. They are the bonds of connections with our fellow man. Human beings are so constructed that they need one another. The giving and receiving of gifts reinforces those bonds that make our lives meaningful.

Fourth Result: We learn and grow

We learn and grow when we give. We cannot learn the value of any material thing until we give it away. Now we do not value material things just because of their monetary worth. We also prize many items because of their sentimental value as it is called. We may treasure photographs for the images of the persons they have captured. We may treasure rather useless items because they were given to us. The pictures, the trifling gifts teach us the meaning of material things: they represent the love and relationship we have with other people. Take away those items and we have not changed the relationship; we simply have lost a reminder of it. Human beings instinctively know the true value of items. A poor woman living in the hills is not likely to trade her wedding ring for a brand new expensive jewel. The ring means more than money. The mother will not throw away the last letter her son wrote to her, although the words were not spelled correctly and it was smudged with ink. That is why the most valuable gifts anyone can give are gifts that are invested with one's self. True giving teaches us this most important lesson — all giving, to be true giving, must be self-giving.

We grow through giving. As we learn to use and give material objects we grow to maturity in our thinking. We also slowly give up all things. Human life is a process of acquiring and losing. We come into the world totally helpless and with absolutely nothing. Through our lives we collect item after item, objects and clothing, degrees and experiences, jobs and promotions, houses and cars, land and property. And then, slowly in some cases, faster in others, we lose all these things. Our health deserts us, we retire or lose our jobs, we can no longer enjoy our property, we leave our money to our children, at the end we cannot even enjoy food. Coming to terms with material things is closely related to what happens in life.

Fifth Result: Happiness and joy come to us

We are most joyful when we give. If we are forced to give, we give sadly, but that is not true giving. True giving means that we give joyfully, and our joy grows with giving. It is rare to find a person who regrets giving. Some persons may find that the cause to which they gave much turned out to be a false cause, or the persons who took care of the money squandered and misused it. And this may be the source of disappointment or even anger. Yet the joy they had experienced on giving was true joy and that experience was valid. We feel happy when we give, sometimes because we see the joy on the faces of the recipients. At other times, we are not present to see their joy, but we still feel a deep interior peace. Giving to others brings out the best of us. When we can give, our hearts expand. As we give more, our hearts expand more. It is like the effect of heat and air. They expand to fill the room.

Christmas Giving

Christmas is the time of the year when we think most about giving. But we all know that Christmas giving is not easy. In some cases it is problematic. In other cases, it is truly a chore, and one that we might wish to be free of.

But Christmas, like no other time, reminds us of the importance of gift-giving. A child might ask, "If it's Jesus' birthday, why do we give gifts to each other, and not to him?"

Some of us have grown so world-weary that we don't even ask this question, much less think of the response. But, of course, we give gifts to each other on Christmas because of Jesus. He gave us love and the example of giving out of love. And he specifically told us that what we do for one another, is done for him. We give gifts to each other on Christmas because his love teaches us to do so.

Christmas is the time when we are often reminded that it is far better to give than to receive. Children never quite believe that. If they have been taught well, they take joy in buying or preparing gifts for their families, but they still go to bed wondering what Santa Claus will have for them.

Adults who have long since given up on Santa may no longer think about what he may bring, and they no longer care whether they receive one more tie, one more blouse, or one more household or sport appliance. They spend their time hurriedly buying gifts for everyone else and hoping that the others will like what they bought.

What should be a joyous and free exchange of gifts becomes, in many cases, a burden, but one that there is no easy way out of.

All of us need to rethink Christmas and not allow storekeepers and commercials on television or in the newspaper to decide what we should do. It seems that a few gifts, given with more care and love, would be better than flooding the living room with them. But this cannot be done without a complete understanding on the part of the whole family.

We need to start with the children. Many parents, scrapped for money, use Christmas as a way to give the children what they would have given them anyway. Children catch on to this, especially when the gifts are mostly clothes or needed items for school. Parents could handle this in more than one way. Since kids understand this, allow their gifts to be the needed items at Christmas (it does give them more packages to open and often the surprise element is still there, if parents foresee future needs). Or they may simply tell their children that such items will be given as needed. Christmas gifts, as true gifts, will be separate. They will be gifts, either lovingly chosen, or preferably homemade for the child.

Children will be encouraged to make gifts for their parents. One little handmade gift must be appreciated more than quantities of store-bought gifts, unless the child has worked very hard to earn the money for such gifts.

But before such elements work, we really need to become convinced that it really is the thought that counts, not the amount of money that is spent. And in the United States we simply don't believe that. Our commercials repeat over and over again — the expensive item is better; the expensive item says that we care (enough to send the very best!).

Yet it must be said that there is room to be extravagant. After all, Jesus himself gave us the most beautiful examples of extravagant giving in his own life. He also allowed it as in the case of the woman, the well-known sinner, who came and poured perfume over his feet. The apostles were shocked. This could have been sold and the money given to the poor. No, Jesus said, allow her to show her love in that extravagant manner. There is a time and a place for it.

So too at Christmas. At least occasionally we should be totally extravagant — give the truly elegant gift, buy the item that the other wanted and never thought he would get. Take an extra job and work hard just to have more to give. There is a time and place for such actions.

But at Christmas we cannot be concerned just about giving to our own families, our own friends. As Jesus said, even the pagans do that. It is for us to also give to the poor, the lame, the sick, those who wander down the lanes and the byways. To give to them at Christmas is to truly give in the manner in which the babe of Bethlehem gave. It is significant that those who were called to the stable were the shepherds, poor unlettered folk, as well as the three kings, no doubt of another culture and another religion.

We will make our Christmases truly joyful if we remember what Christmas is all about. And we cannot do that if we feel too burdened. We have to let go of all nonessentials and concentrate on what is important. And what is important includes giving to the poor and the helpless.

Now many people do give to the poor at Christmas.

The problem is that they ignore the poor the rest of the year. What is needed is an atmosphere of Christmas all year long.

The Gifts That God Gives Us

God has most abundantly endowed us with gifts. He has given us life and a wonderful world to live it in. He has given us family and friends, work and enjoyment. He has filled our lives with more than we could ever use or need.

But He has not stopped there. He has endowed us with many spiritual gifts, of the type that St. Paul told us about. These gifts are always around us and sometimes, in St. Paul's day as in ours, they are unfortunately the cause of confusion.

Spiritual Gifts

All of these spiritual gifts come to us through the Holy Spirit. We are so dependent, Paul tells us, that we cannot even say, "Jesus is Lord," except through the Spirit (1 Cor 12:3). Paul also tells us that the gifts we are given are given not only, or not especially, for ourselves, but for the Church. They are to be used to build up the Church.

"There is a variety of gifts," Paul says, "but always the same Spirit; there are all sorts of services to be done, but always to the same Lord; working in all sorts of different ways in different people, it is the same God who is working in all of them" (1 Cor 12:4-6).

81

He goes on to say that one may have the gift of preaching, another the gift of instructing, another the gift of faith, or the gift of healing, or the gift of miracles, or prophecy, or of discerning spirits, another the gift of tongues. All of these gifts are gifts of the same Spirit and all are meant to be used for the sake of others.

St. Paul says that although these gifts are valuable, they are nothing compared to love. The greatest, most important gift we could ever have, ever want, or ever need, is love.

We value love, but perhaps we do not value the other gifts as we should.

Gifts of the Holy Spirit

We have long been taught the gifts of the Holy Spirit. Catholics of a previous generation learned them by heart and were able easily to recite them: Wisdom, understanding, counsel, fortitude, knowledge, piety, and fear of the Lord.

Perhaps recitation of them was the most that many could do. What is needed is an understanding of what these are, an appreciation of them, and a desire to have them. For to realize what they are, is truly to want them.

Wisdom

As we get older, we begin to see the value of wisdom, that power of judging rightly and following the soundest course of action, based on knowledge, experience, and understanding. Since such clear judgment requires a certain amount of lived experience, such a gift is rarely given to the young. Unfortunately, many older people also never acquire it. But it is a much needed gift and one that can help the Church and individuals make their difficult decisions. The wise person is the one to whom one can go and seek advice. This person will not simply tell another what to do; his very wisdom precludes that. Instead he will show each side of the issue and allow the other to make his or her own decision. Usually the wise person points out issues and angles that others do not see. Especially he is able to give a view from eternity and spiritual truths related to the problem. No wonder the symbol of wisdom has traditionally been the owl. The owl flies and sees during the night. His bright eyes pierce the darkness, just as the wise person sees beyond our earthly darkness. In many ways, wisdom encompasses the other gifts.

Understanding

The second gift, understanding, is defined as comprehension, or discernment, and wisdom is built upon it. This gift is first concerned with understanding of the things of God. But this gift also gives us the ability to see beneath the surface. It helps us see the many dimensions that exist in all situations. So much of life and the world is so shallow, so superficial. Understanding is needed to cope with problems that arise, but also to relate with others.

"I don't understand you," someone will say, no doubt honestly.

But the conversation should not stop there. Understanding can come with a little effort. Understanding means to look at what has gone before the current situation, at what has contributed to it, at what all the influences have been. If we have understanding, we are able to see things from another's viewpoint. True understanding is never purely intellectual. It is also affective in that through understanding we are compassionate. Our ordinary use of that word expresses it well. "I understand," someone says, pressing our hand. We know that he means that he feels for us as well as knows what we are going through.

Counsel

Counsel too requires compassion. This gift is not merely a matter of giving advice to others. It requires the Spirit to give us insight into the depths of the other person's situation and a discernment of what would be best under the circumstances. It also is the gift of being able to see what will be the results of certain actions, especially in their everlasting repercussions. With the gift of counsel we can truly help others. We do not take over their problem for them, but we are able to reach out to them, perhaps sympathize with them, perhaps shake them up, perhaps weep with them, perhaps laugh with them, and ultimately say the right words which will help them make appropriate decisions.

One of the ways that counsel is defined in the dictionary is "mutual exchange of ideas, opinions; discussion and deliberation." In this sense we have another understanding of counsel as a gift of the Spirit. Today's Church is full of meetings and committees. In the past perhaps, the priest or the bishop made decisions and told others what to do. Today many decisions are determined by committee recommendations, votes, meetings, and caucuses. These gatherings can be anything from dreary boredom to an unabashed power play for control. But we still pray to the Holy Spirit before such meetings and if we truly ask in faith, these meetings can be infused with the gift of counsel, given to all the members of the group, even the weakest and meekest.

Fortitude

Fortitude, the gift listed fourth, is also not refused to the weak or the meek, although the name makes it sound like the gift of the strong. In the violent society in which we live, too often the physically, financially, or socially strong are admired and emulated. But their strength may not be true strength, nor may their actions exemplify true fortitude. Fortitude is not only courage, but also patient endurance. It allows us to face a calamity with strength and perseverance. This is very different from the current idea of courage as mostly physical courage in fighting.

Today the word "wimp" is used as an insult to anyone who is small or weak or even to one who chooses not to fight. This word is often given to persons who are physically weak or frail, both men and women, although it seems more insulting when it is directed at men. Yet those small or frail persons may have a great deal of fortitude. They are able to patiently endure the insults of others without lashing out. They are able to outlast the other. The one who lives by the sword or the gun or his own physical prowess will die by the same. The "wimp" who steps aside will survive.

But this is not easy to do. Fortunately it is a gift from God, given for the asking.

Fortitude is also the gift that is needed to endure the trials one encounters just because one chooses to live his life according to the spirit of the gospels. At times this will be out and out persecution, but most often it will simply be the sneers and contemptuous laughter of those who find such behavior not only incomprehensible, but even stupid. Here is where fortitude, in its sense of endurance, is needed. For such trials are not a matter of a few minutes, but of a lifetime.

Knowledge

The gift of knowledge is also a gift that takes perhaps a lifetime to grow into. It means much more than simply the act of knowing. Knowledge consists in all that has been perceived or grasped by the mind. It includes learning and enlightenment. By this gift of knowledge, God gives insights into spiritual truths. One may receive true knowledge of God, knowledge that he cannot necessarily explain. Nor can he define what he has learned, but his knowledge is real and experiential. This gift is more commonly given than one might suppose. Many people have fleeting glimpses of God. Many have knowledge of Him that they didn't get from books or sermons. God speaks to their hearts and teaches them deep truths.

Piety

Piety, the sixth gift, is one that is rarely talked of today. No one wants, it seems, to be called pious. It is seen as an over-religious viewpoint, or perhaps a better-than-thou attitude. But of course that is not the true meaning of this virtue. The concept of piety involves the idea of devotion to religious duties and practices. It means delving into their true meaning and finding one's joy and enthusiasm in worship and prayer. One echoes the words of the psalmist: "How I love your temple, O Lord. My delight is to be with you" (see Ps 84).

Piety also includes the idea of loyalty and devotion to the Church as a people as well as the place. A pious person is not someone making display of his prayers and time in church. He is one who loves and cares for the Church and its people.

Fear of the Lord

Finally there is fear of the Lord. We speak less today of fear of God than we once did. Today we like to think in terms of a loving God. Didn't the New Testament, we say, show us the God of love rather than the God of fear? But this gift is not encouraging us into a servile fear of God. It is the loving fear of not wanting to offend, of being aware of the majesty of God, of never losing the profound respect and reverence we have for Him. It is the awe we would have if we saw the burning bush and heard a voice telling us to remove our shoes for we were on holy ground.

What reverence we would have. But at the same time, would not our hearts burn within us at our contact with God?

Fear is not that far from love. Only the servile, cringing fear of the slave is out of line.

All of these gifts are spiritual gifts given to us in the depths of our souls, but manifested in our outer behavior. They by no means limit the gifts of God.

Other Gifts from God

God gives countless gifts, every day delighting us with little surprises. But often His gifts come to us through other people. In a strange way it seems that each person who comes into our lives gives us a gift, often one we would not expect.

This is true even from persons we do not find congenial. We may meet someone who comes across as harsh and uncaring, and yet, from that person we are likely to learn something. That person may be harsh, but he may also have mastered the ability to complete his work efficiently.

Perhaps his gift to us is the lesson of efficient work, which can be done without the harshness. Or we may meet someone who takes nothing seriously, even things we think should be taken very seriously. We can learn from that person at least to question our own seriousness. Gifts are given all around us, everywhere. All of these gifts come from God although they are often in rather unattractive wrapping paper. It would be a pity to reject the gift because we don't like the paper it is wrapped in.

Examples of Giving

It is not hard to find examples of giving people. In fact, everyone we know who has been acclaimed and admired by members of the Church was a giver. This is obvious since giving is one of the hallmarks of a saintly person. The Christian giver is the Christian lover and that is the sign of a relationship to God. Even so, some are more outstanding as givers than others.

Mother Teresa

Through the centuries we can find many persons who gave consistently without counting the cost. Even today there are many. A shining example is Mother Teresa of Calcutta.

She was always a loving giving person, but in India she found her true calling, to care for the most abandoned. She started simply — just to offer those dying in the streets a place to experience some loving care in the last days or hours of their lives. But, as usually happens, the more she loved and cared, the larger her heart became, and the more she reached out to people with all kinds of needs. Now houses where her sisters work are found around the world, and not just in Third World countries. She has also identified the deep needs of the human heart to be found in First World countries.

Mother Teresa rarely speaks publicly and writes little. Those are not her callings. She is simply a loving tender caregiver; nothing is too lowly for her.

What a powerful image she is for the many who are called to give in inconspicuous ways. Mother Teresa herself never calls attention to herself. She is apolitical and uninterested in larger movements. She simply wants to serve.

She relates how as she worked in India teaching at a rather elite girls' school, she saw all around her the poor and the dying. She knew she could not ignore them. She even left her community to start her own which would serve those in need.

But she did not publicly criticize her previous community. She was much too loving for that. She simply saw a need and responded.

As we walk down our streets in the United States, we may not see people dying there, but if we have our eyes open, we will certainly see needy people. And we need to be alert to the nudges of the Spirit as to how we should respond.

St. Vincent de Paul

· Another saint, one who lived a few centuries ago and who saw needs and responded, was St. Vincent de Paul. He grew up poor, so he had experienced poverty firsthand. But he was enormously gifted and naturally charming and delightful to be with. He was able to persuade almost anyone simply through the magnetism of his personality. With such gifts, he could easily have fallen prey to the temptation to serve in a rich parish where he would be loved and admired.

Instead he turned his charm to persuading the wealthy to
help the poor.

Daniel-Rops remarks:

> "The power of charity! But there was more to it
> than that. Vincent was not only an emotional and
> sensitive man, moved to the depth of his being by
> pity; he was not merely an orator — to tell the
> truth he could hardly be called an orator at all.
> Able to move audiences deeply, he was a man of
> action and achievement; an organizer, quick to
> seize a proffered opportunity and to both cause
> and transform into practical action the feelings in
> the hearts of other men and women."

He soon had the well-to-do spending their Sunday
afternoons visiting and providing food and clothing for the
poor. But he knew that such work would not last without
organization and he quickly had these visitors become well-
disciplined groups so that no one would be neglected and
that works of charity would not depend upon whim and
fleeting feelings of kindness.

But Vincent was not just a philanthropist. He really
cared about people. When he heard of human suffering
or pain, he felt something of the sorrow. His compassion,
in the true sense of "suffering with," was real. He did not
love humanity in the abstract; he loved real human beings, flesh and blood, joyful and suffering, miserable and
miraculous.

Love, he said, should be effective as well as affective.
With affective love, we feel for the other person; with
effective love we reach out to them.

St. Francis de Sales

Francis de Sales lived around the same time as Vincent de Paul. In contrast to Vincent he was of a noble family and had every opportunity in life. It is no wonder that he quickly was appointed a bishop and that he was sent to head the see of Geneva. But Geneva at that time was the center of the Calvinist reformation and Catholics were not welcome in many circles.

But Francis, like Vincent, was a gentle loving person. He lived and practiced a personal religion of love. He was not known so much for his charitable giving to the poor as Vincent was, but rather for his giving of loving words and thoughtful actions for others. He stressed a religion of love rather than fear, a concern for the spirit rather than the letter of the law. He did not feel it necessary to preach out against Calvinists; all he needed to do, he believed, was show Christ's love to the world.

Soon, his biographer Bedoyere writes, "he was everywhere in demand as preacher and personal advisor in matters of the spirit. There were other great spiritual men in Paris at that date, but the people were captivated by this combination of spiritual freshness addressed to the hearts of all, united as it was with gentleness, graciousness, affability, geniality, a *doucer* which was neither soft nor sentimental and that seemed connatural to this young and impressive figure. His personality made its immediate mark."

He encouraged people to work for the little virtues: patience, helping their neighbors, service, humility, gentle courage, affability, tolerance of their own imperfections.

St. Francis de Sales is an excellent example for our own day of the kind of service that is open to all of us. We cannot all do things that will be noticed and honored everywhere, but we are all capable of and called to the so-called little virtues.

St. Francis of Assisi

Going back now to the thirteenth century we find that most incredible Francis, the little poor man of Assisi, who chose to take Jesus literally when he told us how to live.

Francis reached out to everyone, but he is especially noted for the way he reached out to those whom others would have ignored: beggars and lepers, for example.

While he was still working at his father's clothing shop, a beggar came in. Francis, who was selling cloth to some wealthy patrons, and who detested both the looks and the smell of the beggar, sent him away. But his conscience would not let him rest. Who was it he had sent away — it was God Himself. Francis ran after the beggar, begged his forgiveness, and filled his hands with coins.

Later, Francis became a knight and rode off dressed in rich armour and garments. He met a knight returning in rags, one who had not only lost in battle, but had lost the respect of his people. Francis took off his rich cloak and gave it to the poor man so that he could at least return home respectably. Francis had the touch of knowing and responding to the material needs of people, but he was concerned with their emotional needs too.

He not only gave food and clothing to lepers, but, knowing how lepers were treated and thought of in his society, he washed the lepers' wounds and kissed them.

Once when one of his little brothers cried out in the night from hunger because he was unused to the long fasts, Francis gave him food, and then broke his own fast to eat

with him. He would not have this little brother lose heart,
nor think that he was unworthy of the life of the brotherhood.

Francis also knew that givers need to be loved as well
and so he accepted to eat whatever was given to him as he
begged.

Francis' love extended not only to human beings, but
even to animals. He loved all of creation. He was daily
delighted with the dawn of the brilliant sun and with the
gentle glow of the moon and the stars. He loved the winds
blowing through the valleys, the rain which watered the
earth, the trees which grew on the hillsides, the mountains
which seemed to reach to God, the valleys which provided
quiet seclusion. Francis was so in love with God that he loved
all that God had made and he never failed to show it to all.
The world was full of gifts, as Francis saw, and he responded
by giving all he had.

Other Examples

We need not look to canonized or acclaimed saints to
find examples of giving. They are all around us: parents
who give unstintingly for their families, friends who will
come to your aid even when you don't ask for it, even
strangers who give generously to help someone in need.
Even the earth generously gives more than we could ever
use.

Cynicism Related To Giving

It is easy to be cynical about giving, especially so-called professional giving. Rich people give money so that they can write it off their taxes. People go to $1000-a-plate dinners to support their favorite charity, but they make sure that they are noticed by the press as they go. People attend an elegant fund-raising affair to raise money for the poor, who are never, under any circumstances, invited to such functions.

Or people give gifts only to receive gifts in return. Or fund-raisers write the most tear-jerking letters in which they include horrendous pictures of children starving in Africa in order to get us to send them money to feed the poor. But we find out later that much of that money never reaches the poor. It goes instead for the administration of the project, including paying those writers who have written such letters.

When one goes abroad in certain countries one may find himself surrounded by poor children. It is hard to resist giving to such children — until we find that they take the money that has been given to them and give it to some older well-nourished and well-dressed man who stands in the background.

One could easily become cynical.

But it is overwhelmingly important not to.

For giving is what we must do. We must remember that

we do not give just because the other person is needy, but because we have the need to give. Certainly we should not throw our money away foolishly. Nor is it right to encourage children to become beggars, nor others to become dependent. What is needed is a generous heart which is as gentle as a dove, but as wise as a serpent.

There are ways of giving in which cynicism is lessened. When we give generously of our time and effort to those around us, we are less likely to become cynical. After all, these are our family and we love them. But often family members, mothers especially, feel that their families take them for granted and expect all that self-giving. Here, too, one needs to guard against cynicism and becoming discouraged.

Giving must be generous and voluntary. When it becomes a duty or obligation it is not real giving. When we feel that it is expected, our freedom and joy in giving are curtailed. Thus the wise mother of a family will not allow the others to take her for granted. From childhood on, she will teach her children to express gratitude and to do their share of the work. This is more difficult in many cases than simply doing it herself.

A generous and giving attitude in a family can be cultivated along the lines of "I don't work for you; you don't work for me. We are a family and we work to support each other."

It is paramount if one feels that he or she is doing all the giving to talk about the problem. Otherwise the giving will not only be cynical but bitterness will develop.

Psychologists have often pointed out that family members do not talk to each other enough, particularly about the things that bother them. They talk about the weather, the neighbors, the news, even politics, before they are willing to broach the subject of "I am being treated unfairly!"

On the larger level, we must also make efforts to avoid cynicism. We know we need to give, but how are we to decide to whom we should give when so many begging letters arrive each day and each one seems so urgent? We certainly need to make some choices and we would do well to do some research to find those which most fit our response. Once that is done, we can respond to some and throw other letters in the waste basket, without feeling either guilty or cynical. To say that some money is wasted or misused or lines the pockets of an already well-off person cannot be used as an excuse to eliminate all giving. All charitable organizations cannot be tarred with the same brush. We give our money to organizations that we must trust to help the poor. And if we can, we should get involved enough that we, too, make decisions as to the use of the money.

If giving money to charity arouses cynicism, so too does working with the needy. They may not be responsive or grateful; they may not even like us. Or they may take advantage of us, or as often happens, they will steal from us even as we minister to them. Again we cannot allow our charity to become cynical. We must just learn to evaluate the situation. We know that when we give, when we put ourselves in the role of giver, we are assigning the other to be receiver, a subordinate position. Most people do not like to be subordinate; they will find ways to equalize the situation. Understanding that helps prevent cynicism.

So does looking again at our intentions. Our purpose must be to help others rather than to reap rewards.

Thoughts On Gifts and Giving

Some of these thoughts are very Christian in approach; others are less so. Some are filled with deep understanding of human nature; others are simply cynical. Still they may all provide some interesting thoughts and discussion.

Gifts:

"The only gift is a portion of thyself . . . the poet brings his poem; the shepherd his lamb . . . the girl, a handkerchief of her own sewing." (Ralph Waldo Emerson)

"The gift . . . must be the flowing of the giver unto me, correspondent to my flowing unto him."
(Ralph Waldo Emerson)

A gift is . . . "the merest trifle set apart from honest gains, and sanctified by faith." (Mahabharata)

"Gift are like fish-hooks." (Martial)

"A synonym of trade." (Austin O'Malley)

A gift . . . "consists not in what is done or given, but in the intention of the giver or doer." (Seneca)

"A bribe with bells." (John Steinbeck)

"Whatever man has." (Christopher M. Wieland)

Giving:

Giving is . . . "social action." (William Bolitho)

"The only thing we ever have." (Louis Ginsberg)

"The business of the rich." (Johann W. Goethe)

"One glorious chain of love." (Samson R. Hirsch)

"When I give I give myself." (Walt Whitman)

Giving is . . . "not giving beyond the possibility of return." (Anon.)

Charity:

"A virtue of the heart, not of the hands."
(Joseph Addison)

"The perfection and ornament of religion."
(Joseph Addison)

"A helping hand stretched out to save men from the inferno of their present life." (William Booth)

"The love of God for himself, and our neighbor for God." (Thomas Browne)

"Organized charity is doing good for good-for-nothing people." (Elizabeth Barrett Browning)

"A disciple having asked for a definition of charity, the Master said, 'Love One Another.' " (Confucius)

"This only is charity, to do all, all that we can." (John Donne)

"A private concern." (Barry M. Goldwater)

"Something saved from frivolity." (Norman Greene)

"To squander . . . superfluous wealth on those to whom it is sure of doing the least possible good." (William Hazlitt)

"The spice of riches." (Hebrew Proverb)

"The sterilized milk of human kindness." (Oliver Herford)

"No man giveth, but with intention of good to himself; because gift is voluntary, and of all voluntary acts the object is to every man his own good." (Thomas Hobbes)

Charity is . . . "a thing that begins at home and usually stays there." (Elbert Hubbard)

"A debt of honor." (Immanuel Kant)

"Universal benevolence whose fulfillment the wise carry out conformably to the dictates of reason so as to obtain the greatest good." (Gottfried W. Leibnitz)

"The bone shared with the dog when you are just as hungry as the dog." (Jack London)

"Helping a man to help himself." (Moses Maimonides)

"A matter on which the immediate effect on the persons directly concerned, and the ultimate consequences to the general good, are apt to be at complete war with one another." (John Stuart Mill)

"All mankind's concern." (Alexander Pope)

"The perfection of the Christian life . . . which in some sort unites or joins man to his God." (Pope John XXIII)

"(That which) opens in each heart a little Heaven." (Matthew Price)

"A naked child, giving honey to a bee without wings." (Francis Quarles)

"A gift of God, and when it is rightly ordered, likens us to God himself, as far as that is possible; for it is charity which makes the man." (St. John Chrysostom)

. "(That which) deals with symptoms instead of causes." (Herbert Samuel)

"To help the feeble up and support him after." (adapted from William Shakespeare)

"Money put to interest in the other world." (Robert Southey)

"Whatever capital you divert to the support of shiftless and good-for-nothing persons." (William G. Sumner)

"The desire to be useful to others without thought of recompense." (Emanuel Swedenborg)

"To will and to do what is just and right in every transaction." (Emanuel Swedenborg)

"(That which) equals all the other commandments." (Talmud: Baba Bathra, 9a.)

"Friendship to all the world . . . friendship expanded like the face of the sun when it mounts above the eastern hills." (Jeremy Taylor)

"Essentially it is a mere act of justice." (William Temple)

"With one hand I take thousands of dollars from the poor, and with the other I hand back a few dimes."
(Leo Tolstoy)

"Christian charity is the supernatural virtue of the love for God insofar as it extends from God to our fellow men." (Eberhard Welby)

"A religious duty." (Louis Wirth)

"A disguise for the injustice that we mete out to our fellow men." (Ida A. Wylie)

"Good will is the best charity." (Yiddish Proverb)

"A magnet with more power to attract the divine influence than any other precept." (Shneor Zalman)

Bibliography

Bedoyere, Michael de la, *Francois de Sales*. New York: Harper & Row, 1960.

Brussell, Eugene E. (ed.) *Dictionary of Quotable Definitions*. Englewood Cliffs, N.J.: Prentice-Hall, 1970.

Daniel-Rops, Henri, *Monsieur Vincent*. New York: Hawthorne, 1961.

Gittins, Anthony J., *Gifts and Strangers*. New York: Paulist Press, 1989.

Green, Julien, *God's Fool*. New York: Harper & Row, 1983.